P9-CQZ-165

The Small World of Long-Distance Sailors

The Small World of Long-Distance Sailors

by ANN CARL

A Triton Book

DODD, MEAD & COMPANY

New York

To
Bill, captain of *Audacious*

The story of modern argonauts who have chosen, for various reasons, to live in the small world of a sailboat, and who continually crisscross one another's paths as they sail long distances between far-flung harbors of the world...

Portions of this book have previously appeared in *Yachting* magazine.

Published by Dodd, Mead & Company, Inc.
79 Madison Avenue, New York, N.Y. 10016
Distributed in Canada by
McClelland and Stewart Limited, Toronto
Manufactured in the United States of America
First Edition

Library of Congress Cataloging in Publication Data

Carl, Ann.
The small world of long-distance sailors.

"A Triton book."
1. Sailing. I. Title.
GV811.C338 1985 797.1'24 84-24687
ISBN 0-396-08519-9 (pbk.)

Contents

Acknowledgments

Writing about real people presents certain responsibilities. All the people met in this book are real, and I have strived to picture them strictly as we knew them, with quotations derived from careful notes taken at the time. For any misquotations, I offer an apology; they are certainly unintentional. Inevitably, there are a few people who are presented in an unfavorable light, and these I have not mentioned by name.

It has been a privilege to be a part of this fraternity of long-distance sailors (even those un-named), and we continue to look for you in every harbor we enter, even as we encounter new recruits.

It was Tony Gibbs, former editor of *Yachting* magazine, Spencer Smith of Dolphin Book Club, Douglas Logan of Dodd, Mead, and Jack Tebbel, editor and writer, who encouraged me to write a book about this strange new breed of sailor. My husband Bill sacrificed many hours of my sanding and varnishing time on the boat to this project, and he patiently corrected sailing terms and pointed out errors in boat drawings.

Argonauts

Out of a life seeming suddenly
 overpolled, overextolled, over-overseen
 polluted, computerized, too populated
 tinny, noisy, and pornographic
 greedy, goal-less and threatening holocaust
certain renegades set forth.

Out of this stifling tedious contest
 into a new and unknown maelstrom
 into unleashed winds and building waves
 on a shifting, indifferent, uncaring sea
 in a fragile sail-powered cockleshell
these modern argonauts risk all.

Out upon the wild and open sea
 bows pointed to strange lands, strange harbors
 encountering currents unforeseen, uncharted reefs
 encountering calms, beating sun and rainbows
 encountering others, time and time again, around the globe
fellow searchers, sailing all together.

Out upon the salty, far-off, lonely highways
 out of reach of foreboding newscast
 out of touch with changing mores and fashions
 the absolute, utter reality looks back
 stares silently, unflinchingly, unanswering
and still these sailormen keep on—
 looking for the safe harbor of golden sunset
 looking for the company of like men.

The Small World of Long-Distance Sailors

I

A Multitude of Sailors

A man with wet gray hair and hands not yet toughened enough to be comfortable hauling in cold, sea-drenched sheets, braces himself at the wheel of his newly acquired boat and peers into the darkness ahead. The wind has risen and the trip he had thought would be short and easy is now a struggle, with strong seas rolling in out of the night and sails cracking and pulling in too much wind.

Below, his wife tucks towels around dishes, radios, and books to keep them from rolling repeatedly onto the cabin sole. Waves crash against the hull, boil down the deck, and run off the stern.

Already, the man is tired and fearful, his wife nervous, probably resolving never to get into a sailboat again.

The man's eyes are clouded with the seawater cutting through them as he tries to see the harbor buoy ahead. In the back of his mind is the knowledge that foreign countries often do not keep buoys lighted. It may be there, but he might never see it.

"Can you get the beacon on the radio now?" he calls into the wind to his wife.

She goes to the radio, allowing pillows and books to fall again.

"Can you get the beacon?" he calls again.

"I'm trying. I'm trying. There's still too much static." Then, "I think I have it. There's something. I'll try for a bearing."

"What?"

She does not answer but works for a bearing on the radio beacon at Messina.

She goes to the companionway.

"You are heading about ten degrees to the left," she says.

"I can't hold any higher. I'll have to take down the jib. You'll have to steer."

She hates to do it, but clutches the wheel while he goes forward and wrestles the sail down. In the dark, she cannot see what he is doing, or whether he is still there.

"Do you have a safety belt on?" she calls out.

No answer, but the sail begins to flog.

"Head into the wind. Into the wind."

She heads toward the waves. The boat seems to stop dead. The black waves toss the small ship; the gleaming foam slashes at her in the cockpit. Finally, the sail is furled and he returns to the cockpit, dripping and breathing heavily. Back on course with the engine on, and with mainsail alone, she points nearer the beacon, the tall mast bobbing in the low clouds.

"I see a light! There's a light!" She points ahead.

And it is indeed the flashing harbor buoy. The radio now has a strong signal from the beacon, straight ahead. It is just a matter of time now, a piece of cake. Already, both minds are picturing the act of tying up the boat to the mole, of going below into the lighted (and still) cabin, eating, and finally crawling into the bunk to sleep. The gnawing fear of searching for a big unlit buoy somewhere in the reeling, noisy darkness, and of feeling the boat overpowered by the wind and sea, suddenly turns into a sense of accomplishment, of being one with the ancient sailors and working boatmen of this foreign land.

Private little dramas like this are taking place every day, every night, in every part of the globe, as former engineers, physicians, real estate brokers, students, artists—people from all walks of life—are taking to the sea in small boats with only their wives or girl friends as crew. Sometimes, it is true, such dramas do not end as happily as this, and boats are lost, their fate forever a mystery. But, surprisingly, after a little sailing experience, the proper lessons are learned and this new long-distance sailing fraternity proceeds about the world.

There is still a good deal of controversy as to exactly *why* there

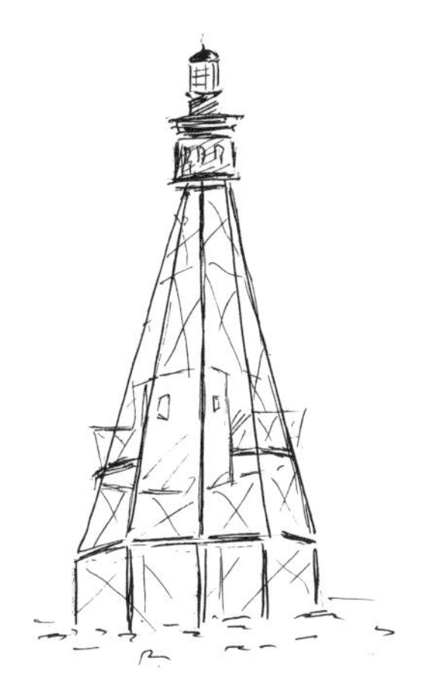

Skeleton Island Lighthouse

has been this sudden exodus to the sea—and in this look at many of these travelers, we will have members of this new breed speak for themselves about that—but it is easy to see how they are *able* to do it.

Look at any sailing magazine (it does not matter in what country) and you will find pictured there boats of every size that are said to be able to cross any sea in homelike comfort. They are seaworthy, with strong hulls, self-bailing cockpits, masts and sails rigged for stiff weather and fast sailing. Also described is equipment like that used on big ships for navigating long distances and in the worst weather conditions. Finally, there are self-steering devices to allow the crew and skipper to sleep while the boat sails on. And interspersed throughout are titillating pictures of south sea passages, or, for the more rugged, storm-tossed shores of the frigid north, to set a sailor dreaming. He begins to wonder why he cannot do something that men, and even girls, have been doing single-handed, when he, after all, will have a crew to help.

It is not long before the dreaming armchair sailor begins to make real plans. He no longer can lean back on any excuse not to, and he begins to look tentatively around for the proper boat for his trip. He goes to the boat shows and walks around on various boats, trying out the feel of the wheel (he sees Tahiti's palms ahead) and criticizes the lack of space in the galley. He collects books and reads how it is out in the Atlantic, where the good ports in the Mediterranean are, how to plan for getting money and mail abroad. Finally, he gets some charts and spreads them out on the living room floor.

If anyone finds him there, he just says casually, "Well, I might sail a boat over here to Greece." His friends laugh at such an idea. Meanwhile, his wife watches with consternation.

Still, it is not hard to imagine a retiree with a long background of sailing deciding to set sail for the far oceans. Even his wife would not be too surprised at the suggestion. And many of this new breed of ocean-crossing sailors are just that–retirees who are still strong and alert, now taking, at last, that dream voyage to faraway isles. It is a final test of one's knowledge and experience, and a challenge (rather than a long vacation) in the retirement years.

This is, in fact, where *we* now fit into the picture. Bill designed hydrofoil ships and windmills for power at Grumman Aerospace Corporation. I was a science writer and test pilot.

But many of these long-distance crews are young, and many are taking their young children with them. In a way, they, too, are putting themselves to the test, in order to discover what they really want out of the rest of their lives, especially if they have become disenchanted with some aspects of them. They have special problems of logistics–school-age children aboard, for instance, and the wherewithal to finance the venture.

There is a large group comprised of "old sailors who never die." These are sailors caught up in the sailing life for one reason or another, who simply got trapped in it and never learned anything else. A few ultimately become involved in smuggling–human beings or contraband–or in sinister skeins of terrorism, all for quick money, or perhaps for glamor and excitement. They are the low life of the ocean ports, the water rats, thieves, and criminals. Every port is cursed with them.

But, fortunately, not all the "sailors for life" are suspect. Most are energetic and expert and have found useful careers in sailing. Take the delivery crews. They are in charge of boats of all sizes and ages, bound for every destination. Usually there is an experienced captain, a neophyte crew or two, and perhaps a girl or two as cook or stewardess. They have little to say to other sailors, except to other delivery crews, and they are very competitive. Their greatest pleasure is in sailing fast new boats on record-setting passages. Those who are employed by well-known boat-delivery agencies do best.

Many who tire of delivery–or sales, or racing, or who simply need money–go into the charter-boat business. Many winter charterers in the Caribbean move to the Mediterranean in the summer, staying constantly on the go. A new expertise is required in this sailing job—dealing with people. Many sailors prefer confronting storms at sea alone to that.

Finally, there is an unclassified group. These are people who simply decide to go to sea. Some might want the challenge, or a simpler, more basic, more economical life. Others might just want to get away and be masters of their own world on their own boats far away from land. There are different reasons in different countries. In some Eastern countries, in fact, sailing has proved to be the only way to freedom.

As we sailed from America to Europe, throughout the Mediterranean, and back to the West Indies, we were astonished at the variety of sailors we found out on the seas in small boats. Because we had all, somehow, overcome storms at sea, malfunctioning engines or sails, navigational surprises, shortages of food or dollars, or attacks by thieves, there was a bond between us. Conversation came easily. Serious questions were discussed and answered, and with more penetration and honesty than they might have been if asked, say, within the dining rooms of some vacation spot.

Confined in the small world of a sailboat at sea, sailors see a lot, contemplate a lot. And it is surprising to find how small the planet seems when these boats keep coming upon one another in ports around the world.

II

Ocean Passage—A Requirement

It is understood that those who would become qualified members of the long-distance sailing fraternity commit themselves to at least one transoceanic crossing. ("Hum" Barton made twenty-two Atlantic crossings in all, in boats smaller than forty feet—but we will meet him later, in Malta.)

These candidates must have reached an understanding between themselves and the sea and be ready to take whatever the sea gives them. They will have learned that the sea is a totally indifferent entity, powered by the forces of wind and weather and ocean current, where ships and sailors intrude upon their own responsibility. If they, instead, have a lingering hope that the sea can be placated or can be indulgent in any way, they will have to learn the truth on some bleak night of storm when the wind's howl has no end, when the boat creaks and tosses and refuses to respond, and still the wind and sea continue their fury.

"The ocean knows no favorites," Samuel Eliot Morison wrote. "Her bounty is reserved for those who have the wit to learn her secrets, the courage to bear her buffets, and the will to persist, through good fortune and ill, in her rugged service."

But one cannot commit oneself—and one's family, one's boat, and, often, one's friends and their children—to the long ocean passages lightly.

The selection of the proper boat is of first importance. Of course it must be within the owner's means—but then, most sailors ready to spend years at sea have sold their houses so that the proper boat can be bought. After all, it is to be their sole home for a long time—possibly forever.

Consider first what some of the very experienced cruising sailors look for in a boat. Lin and Larry Pardey chose *Serrafyn* (had her built just for their circumnavigation) for her seaworthiness and simplicity of operation—no engine, no mechanical heads, no electronics, but lots of stowage and room to work, on deck and below. They sailed aboard her for eleven years before deciding upon a new boat, which is only four feet longer, is still wood, and still has no engine or electronics. And they are building it themselves.

New Zealanders Eric and Susan Hiscock, after fourteen years with a steel boat and forty years of worldwide sailing, have returned again to wood, and have gone from fifty feet back to thirty-nine. Besides good performance to windward in big seas, they want things like full-length cockpit seats for outdoor sleeping in the tropics.

Most Europeans, who have heavy-weather sailing grounds like the North Sea and the English Channel, the Mediterranean and Pentland Firth (where the strongest currents in the world can flow) prefer a cockpit protected with a hard deckhouse on their cruising boats.

One Englishman we met was even more specialized. He had built his own forty-seven-foot fiberglass ketch for world cruising—with only two berths.

"Any guests who want to sail with us," he said, "are welcome to day-sail, but they will stay in hotels at night. That way we stay friends."

Today's American market provides a choice between fiberglass racer-cruiser type stock boats and the "sailing condominiums," with every comfort and gadget, but questionable sailing performance. In fact, some traditionalists say the latter sail sideways rather than straight ahead.

But aside from personal design preferences, there are a few basic requirements for any long-distance sailor. Since there is much informed advice available now, we will not try to duplicate it here, except to offer a few cautionary words:

1. *Seaworthiness:* It goes without saying that the vessel for this sort of expedition must be well and truly built for ocean sailing. But just *looking* strong is not enough. Some people have been talked into purchasing heavy craft that cannot perform, cannot push their bulk through oncoming seas or make enough speed to cover the miles to a reasonable destination. On the other hand, some boats that appear flimsy and vulnerable, like *Moxie*, the big fifty-foot trimaran Phil Weld sailed to win the 1980 single-handed OSTAR race, can be designed to be fast and light and responsive enough to laugh at ocean gales. So, most importantly, any decision about a vessel's potential seaworthiness requires analysis, comparing, trying out.

2. *Proper rigging and sails:* Of course, lightweight racing rigging is not proper for extensive long-distance sailing, nor are racing sails. The state of the fastenings is probably more important than the choice of rigging—and plenty of extra fittings should be included in the inventory. Sail inventory should include storm sails, and whether you are partial to one mast or several, a double-head rig (furling Genoa and smaller forestaysail) provides a lot of safety and ease of handling.

3. *Space below:* For LDS (Long Distance Sailing), space for stowage and, ideally, a real workshop, as well as for washing oneself and one's clothes, is far more important than a large number of berths. If you must have guests or a crew (and the longer you live aboard, the less you will), remember that most long passages require sailing in watches, and bunks therefore can be shared.

4. *Inventory:* The most important items are tools—electrical, mechanical, plumbing, and carpenter tools—and spare parts (three of each, not just two). Food and things like toilet paper all narrow down to the number of people times the number of days. Clothes should be kept to the minimum, and washable. Room should be left for foreign articles picked up along the way—it is hard to resist native artifacts. When we met Roy and Rika Gingell's *Honnalee* from Vancouver, she was decorated with spears and masks from the Pacific islands. The Blacks from Seattle had made the cabin of their Valiant-40 *Foreign Affair* as sumptuous as an Arab sheik's tent, with Oriental rugs and cushions from the Middle East.

5. *Navigational equipment:* First, most LDS sailors assume that none of it but the sextant and compass will work when desperately

needed, then choose sparingly the electronics they need. They will ask experienced sailors about their usefulness and dependability before they buy. But perhaps a better buy is a good celestial navigation course and a ham radio for communication with the outside world. With any electronics, it seems to work out best to get the best, not the cheapies, and have them installed by electronics experts.

6. *Charts, guides, lists:* We found it wise not to get charts for worldwide sailing all at once (even if it were possible to afford them, or stow them), nor, on the other hand, to wait to buy them in each country. Instead, it seems best to get them in batches – that is, in the United States, get charts for crossing the Atlantic to your first landfall. Then, in places like London, Gibraltar, and Malta, get the British Admiralty charts for your next two thousand miles or so. Get all the guides – like H. M. Denham's Mediterranean series or the Yachtsman's Guides to the Greater Antilles, the Bahamas, and so on. Read them ahead of time to get a feel of what is ahead. One of the best, though least known, guides to European waters is the series of Royal Cruising Club Folios, available in London. These are kept up to date by members cruising in these waters. Of course, you must have the U.S. Sailing Directions or British Pilots for every region you sail in. But with all these, save room on the bookshelf for paperbacks – for trading material and for making friends!

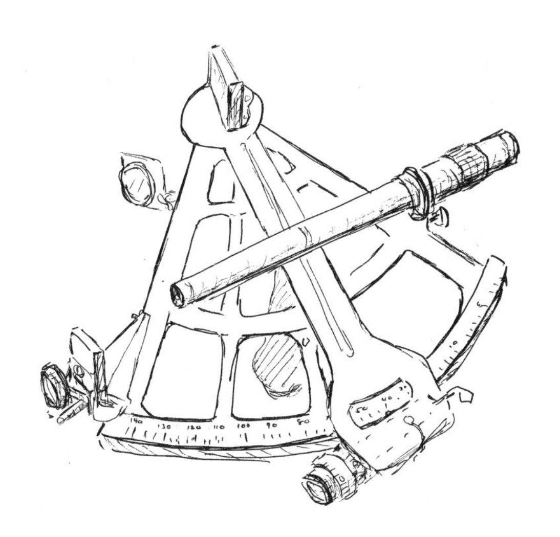

U.S. Navy Sextant

All in all, "tried and true" is not a bad guide when choosing boat or equipment (which perhaps makes it easier than choosing a spouse). We, for instance, decided upon a conservatively designed custom yawl of strip-planked wood construction. She had a roomy aft owner's cabin, a centerboard (her four-foot, three-inch draft made it possible to cruise the French canals; her eight-foot draft with board down gave her seagoing stability), and she had sails of moderate size for two people to handle.

Her lines were fine, and she was beautiful to look at lying at anchor in any harbor. Her name was *Audacious*.

Her Maine designer, Cy Hamlin, and Maine builders, Goudy and Stevens, fashioned a true-blue sailer. She tracked her course and rose comfortably to any sea. She had heart in any storm. To us, and to many LDS sailors, though not all, these qualities are important to the enjoyment of the voyage.

We were selective in buying equipment like refrigeration, radios, and electronics: Adler-Barber cold-plate engine compressor refrigeration; Decca eighty-eight-channel VHF radio (in Europe, different channels are required); Brookes and Gatehouse Heron RDF (with tuning so fine that apparently overlapping stations can be separated); and the prize-winning Northstar LORAN-C. Our ham radio was a Yeasu, with antenna tuner and long-wire antenna (up the mizzenmast and across to the mainmast). We did not have radar, as, financially, we had to choose between it and LORAN. For us, and for most LDS's, a good LORAN-C is more useful, as it is an aid both offshore and inshore. We also decided against OMEGA and satellite navigation systems – OMEGA because in 1977 the stations were not well established and SATNAV because it is sometimes necessary to wait hours before the proper satellite for your position is in place, and because both require constant use of electric power. Of course, it is nice if you can afford them all, plus a weather facsimile machine. In 1977, marine single sideband radio was not widely used abroad, but then we had ham radio SSB capability.

Bill also had a full workshop with power tools, workbench, light, and headroom, plus storage space, under the port cockpit seat. It was reached by a steel ladder from the cockpit. Spare parts, paints, and supplies were segregated in (L. L. Bean) picnic baskets with lids. He had worked out a few special emergency measures, too. From the center cockpit, a quick jerk on a line would release the life ring plus 150 feet of floating line for a man overboard to grab. We had downhauls on all sails, and wire cables along each deck from bow to stern to which each man could hook the line from his own safety harness with a big hook. (Never mind that this made quite a noise rattling along the deck–it meant a man was free to move without refastening.)

The main thing to remember, however, in going on an ocean passage, is that all decisions must have been made before untying the dock lines for the last time. From then on, you and your crew are in your own self-contained world, dependent upon your own ingenuity and adaptability. I remember listening wistfully to all the sounds of land–birds, cars passing, even the insects–the night before we took off across the wide, open Atlantic from Halifax, Nova Scotia.

The crew, too, is now aboard–for better or worse. Considering that the crew may be together on board for three to six weeks, if its members have not been as carefully selected as the equipment, the results can be much worse. We know of one poor captain who took along a good-looking lad he knew very little. When storms seemed to follow one another on their passage, the boy went berserk and had to be sedated and *tied* below. Not only was this extremely distressing, it also made them shorthanded in storm conditions.

William Snaith, in his *Across the Westward Ocean*, said he selected his transatlantic crew on *Figaro* as much for compatibility and what they would add to the ambience–humor, music, cooking and story-telling ability–as for expertise in sailing. Sometimes a marvelously expert crew of sailors, though fine in a race around the buoys, can be marvelously dull on a long voyage. I remember sailing back from Bermuda once, shorthanded but with a crew of "experts." The conversation, from St. David's Light at Bermuda to Newport Harbor, was an agonizing analysis of sail and hull design of every winner of every race known to any of them. It was a relief to have a few birds following along to talk to.

A crew without the "light touch" can be depressing. If one and all must be constantly impressed with the alleged skill and knowledge of one of its members, thoughts of murder follow. In close quarters, if someone begins to feel he is being pushed around or ignored, there is no time to do much chucking under the chin or holding of hands. We once had a crewmember who even defied the captain.

"Suppose I decide what you tell me is not what I think should be done and I don't do it?"

The captain's answer was: "I happen to be captain of this boat, as well as owner, and if there is any insubordination I'll just clap you in irons and put you below." The crew was silent after that – it happened in mid-Atlantic – and he did not engage in any more conversation with the captain.

On the other hand, an even-tempered, adaptable, jolly, hard-working crew member is a never-forgotten pleasure. He helps meld together all the others, and he is asked back again. Peter Zendt, from Long Island, is such a crew, and because of it has been asked aboard boats for about every race and ocean passage you could name.

Once the crew is aboard for the transatlantic passage, and the watches set, a routine develops, with the focus changing toward the boat and keeping her going fast along her course. We had one member aboard, Anthony Clarke, who was getting married in Vermont in a month. During his watch, we had every sail up we could carry. (Actually, he and his father, ex-naval officer Bill Clarke, have an uncanny feel for making a boat go fast.) Pretty soon, the crew begins to fit into the boat, and it seems more spacious than when all first came aboard – with personal gear and our forty boxes of stores. (One crew even brought diving tanks along.) The boat is quieter as well, with the "off" watch asleep below.

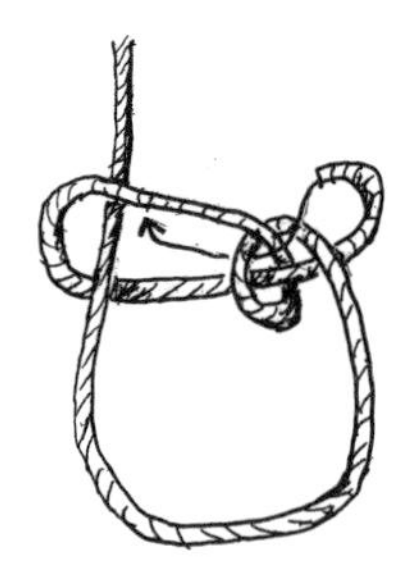

Running Bowline

The day does arrive when everything is packed aboard, the last-minute repairs are finished, the recalcitrant LORAN has been adjusted, and a final photograph of the entire crew in the cockpit has been taken. Docking lines are brought aboard, and the vessel pulls away from the dock, from the land, from the country. Her bow heads out to the open sea.

Each ocean passage is different, and yet the same. Routines and problems are similar, but the luck of the weather and what the crew sees and feels may not be. Our passage from Halifax to Mizen Head, Ireland, was, typically, not spectacular, but had these special events, which other long-distance sailors may well find familiar.

Our course to Ireland was the great-circle course, the shortest for a long ocean passage (it requires a special chart, and a changing course along the way according to the great-circle course formula found in any good navigation textbook). But before setting out upon it, we had to head southeast, below the iceberg limit. The U.S. Coast Guard has charted every berg ever since the sinking of the *Titanic*. We had only to call them to get a position for each one.

We will never know how accurate those plots were, however, for we had dense fog every one of the seventeen days it took us, but one. After blowing the foghorn for the first night, we gave it up. We even stopped peering fearfully ahead and became callous and fatalistic. Sometimes we could pick up engine noise in the ham radio, but we never saw a ship until we got to Ireland. Our world became a gray, wet, shadowy one, whose horizon lay only fifty feet away. The wind, steady and quartering, was strong, and even stronger in the frequent storms. We were entirely dependent upon our ship. We were five small human beings in a wooden shell, apparently not moving inside our closet of fog.

Encouraging us along were the pelagic animals and birds. Dolphins followed us, particularly at night, racing along, sometimes scraping the hull, often squeaking to one another, leaping in explosions of phosphorescence. These creatures and their alien world were only one and a half inches—the thickness of the hull—away.

One evening we met a sperm whale, which passed us closely, small eye watching us. We could smell his rank spume and see his rough gray skin. We kept very still as his seventy-foot hulk moved by us. About two hundred feet astern, he seemed to change his mind, turned sharply, and slapped his huge flukes on the sea, diving in our direction. We waited for a possible collision, but suddenly seven or eight porpoises leaped across his path. We feel they saved us.

Shearwaters and fulmars accompanied us all the way across. Once, a small squadron of sinister, dark skuas came in for an attack on the fulmar population, which was about 150 strong. All day the battles—like airplane dogfights—went on, high in the sky, between the skuas and several scouts from the fulmars. Sometimes the fulmars would cry out and a feather would fall, but in the end the skuas were repulsed, and went away. Fulmars are extraordinarily able fliers.

We baked bread every day. Though in the North Atlantic it takes all day for it to rise enough to bake, the aroma boosts the morale of the crew. On a holiday, we harvested our bean sprouts for a salad, cooked a frozen steak or roast, baked a fruit pie, and drank wine.

On night watches, deep philosophical discussions developed. The secrets of the stars were sought, and old experiences analyzed again.

As we were wrapped in fog, with nothing to see but the gray breaking waves and the ubiquitous fulmars, daily ham radio contact with Joe Lippert in New York gave us the assurance that the rest of the world still existed. To get good radio contact across these thousands of miles is not simple. The boat was not only moving away each day, but was often disappearing below the wavetops. And the radio was operating only on twelve-volt ship's batteries. Joe had started us off with the correct antenna and ground installations. Now he was having to adjust his own antennas to keep us in contact. Some days, weather or propagation conditions would make it impossible.

"In the early summer," he wrote us later, "I used my five band dipole [antenna] which is about 100 feet long, with a transmatch [antenna tuner]. That system could not be directed....When you started to fade in mid-Atlantic, I tried a Gotham ground vertical but it was no good, then a folded dipole on the roof, then the dipole with a reflector element....About midsummer I tried a 'string' beam for 20 meters. It required four ropes into the trees and four aluminum wire elements, covering the front lawn like a giant spider web. It worked surprisingly well....Maybe we could have done better, but I've noticed that contacts over that distance have generally been on a chance basis, but that regular [daily] QSOs [contacts] are rare."

We had had one interesting experience early in the trip that had shown us how surprisingly valuable a ham radio aboard could be. Our first night out from Halifax, still close in to Nova Scotia's southern coast, we had seen flares between us and the mainland. Fearing that someone was in trouble, we wondered what we could do. We elected not to try moving closer to that rocky shore at night, but, rather, to try to interest someone by radio to look for a possible problem there. No one answered my call to "any ship, any plane" on VHF channel 16, the emergency frequency. I tried the ham radio, on eighty meters, hoping for a Canadian response. Two stations answered my emergency alert – one from Michigan and one from Maine. I explained the situation to the Maine station, and very soon an airplane passed over us on a course toward the position of the flares. It seems to be true that there is always someone listening on ham radio who is eager to do some public service.

Our radio contacts with Joe, however, were made in Morse code rather than voice, as we believed the code cut through static and interference better than the human voice. These transmissions were often messages to members of the crew from their families, so when it was difficult to get through, Joe would repeat each word, to be sure, and the messages indeed improved morale aboard ship.

Dividers

Just about the time that the routine of watch, sleep, eat, and struggle in and out of foul-weather gear to go on and off watch began to pall, suddenly we were halfway. We felt we were almost there. We began looking ahead for signs of land, and listening on the radio for European broadcasts.

It was still foggy as we approached the Irish coast – seventeen days out of Halifax – and a gale was blowing. A few large fishing vessels crossed our course but seemed uninterested in our U.S. flag. The LORAN, now set for the Norwegian LORAN chain, had told us at dawn that we were farther along than we felt in our bones we were. (LORAN is notably "iffy" at dawn.) The RDF showed Mizen Head, our landfall, slightly to the north. Then a later LORAN position fell into line with the RDF, and we knew Fastnet was out ahead in the fog. Shortly after dawn, with only three of us on deck – peering ahead, saying nothing – the shifting mists parted enough to show us the solid rock of Mizen Head, then closed in again. Ireland was there! The others came up to see, and gradually we could pick out the line of the coast, then Fastnet Rock with surf breaking against the lighthouse. As we nosed into Long Island Bay, it was as if we had gone through a gray curtain into another world. The sun was shining brightly on Ireland's green, green hills.

We were back from the sea. The long solitary passage – the contest between man and sea, the guardianship and companionship of the boat – was over. It would be a new routine now. Our lives would be governed by the land, its inhabitants, its noises, its regimens. We were strangely silent, rather than exuberant. So it is when a long sea voyage finishes. The strange feeling of loss is what sends the sailor back again and again to the challenge and the mystery of the sea.

III

Sailors of Britain and Eire

When the urgent call from the Admiralty came, they did not hesitate to volunteer either themselves or their boats for the daring rescue attempt.

On May 31, 1940, 242 private boats—ranging in size from twenty-five to eighty-eight feet, sail and motor—sailed in the dense fog from Ramsgate on England's southeastern coast for Dunkirk in France, where Allied troops had been pushed back into the sea by the German army. Admiral Ramsey's "Cockleshell Navy," they were called. But the volunteer boats went in, under cruel air attack, close in to shore, picked up troops until well overloaded, delivered them to troop transports lying offshore, and returned to the confusion and terror of battle again without rest. When, finally, they could do no more, and they took up their course back to England, many boats had been sunk and their owners lost.

Such is the glorious tradition of these seafarers of the northern seas in and around the British Isles.

The word "intrepid" describes them best. It is not by chance that the definitive book *Heavy Weather Sailing* was written by a Britisher (Adlard Coles), for the sailing grounds around the British Isles include no protected bays, like the Chesapeake or Long Island

Sound. When the Britisher goes out to sail, it is to go to sea, and those seas are notoriously stormy. He must learn early how to cope with sudden gales, dense fogs, strong currents, rocky leeward shores, and busy shipping lanes. Over and above the pure skill and perseverance is the inborn pride in being a member of a seafaring nation that calls for extra effort and competency. And we would see yachts flying the British ensigns in ports of every sea.

In fact, in mid-Atlantic, we met a blue yawl flying a British flag coming quietly out of the fog toward us.

"Where are you from?" we called.

"Last port, Ireland," they said, and disappeared again in the fog behind us.

Nowadays, this requirement for good performance at sea is expressed in the designs of British cruising boats. Their boats are stable, usually deep draft, with plenty of sail and tall rigs, but with pretty spartan living quarters. (Their meals are likely to be just as spartan, and it was not too surprising that Laurent Giles suffered from scurvy as recently as a transatlantic race in the seventies – he had subsisted on bully beef and biscuit, made palatable with a little brandy. Sir Francis Chichester grew fresh watercress, at least, on his circumnavigation, though, being a vegetarian, he ate no meat.)

Coming as itinerant long-distance sailors, we entered the British Isles in Ireland, so met the Irish contingent of this rugged sailing race first. They are perhaps more casual than the British, but just as intrepid. The steep, mist-clad cliffs of western Ireland are incessantly battered by Atlantic seas that have come three thousand miles without interruption. The east and north coasts face the temperamental Irish Sea. And both these seas have taken their toll over the centuries of Irish fishermen in their small curraghs.

When we sailed into the open bay of Schull harbor, a basin surrounded by low green hills and neat, patterned fields, there were several brightly colored boats there. Some flew weathered Irish flags, some the various British flags (red ensign for yachts, Blue Peter for members of the services or designated yacht clubs and white for the Royal Yacht Squadron), and a few small ones were French. No one paid the slightest attention to the entering American yacht, even though we had our yellow quarantine flag at the starboard spreader. Some friendly waves were casually acknowledged. A radio call to the harbor master and then to Valencia, the port of entry, brought no answer. Later, we telephoned Valencia and were told simply to "have a good time and don't break any rules." No trouble with papers and inspections here! However, this presented a problem to us, because our crew members could not prove they had landed here by yacht unless someone signed something. But this too was arranged locally, as were hot baths at a hotel later in the day. We did have to wait a few hours for the boiler to heat the water.

Bathed, we had a salmon dinner and joined in a community sing (mostly Stephen Foster songs, oddly enough) in the hotel living room afterward. Other sailors, hotel guests, and Schull local people had all crowded in, most of them sitting on the floor.

We happened to mention that we would like to find a family there by the name of O'Hanna. A Mr. Thompson quickly offered to drive us there. The car was loaded with people, the Irish rain pelted down, and there were many stops. Everyone climbed out to ask directions while standing in the rain and usually getting an answer like: "Well, there are several ways to get there. . . ." But after many turns and tricky climbs along the narrow, rocky roads, we finally did find the O'Hannas. They had bought our house on Long Island in New York and would soon be moving there.

This was the attitude of the Irish toward visiting sailors—friendly, helpful (to a fault), casual, and as likely as not to forget you completely as soon as you were out of sight.

To say they were born to the sea is trite, but true. Even the smallest lad can handle his own curragh. Whole families—each member with his own life preserver, as they do not swim—go off for weeks in a small twenty-foot sailboat in winds that make visiting boats reef and even anchor. They would pass us, all leaning out on the rail, grinning, pink cheeked, and enjoying every minute of it. We happened to anchor in a small harbor at Cape Clear Island with a half dozen of them, plus a few from France. In the morning, out from under the cockpit cover over the boom, climbed families of five or six, plus the family dog.

Perhaps the most notable occasion of Irish cordiality to yachtsmen occurred in 1969 for the celebration of the 250th anniversary of the Royal Cork Yacht Club—purported to be the oldest yacht club in the world, in spite of the fact that it was not always in Cork and is, at present, in Crosshaven. Foreign yachts were invited for a cruise-in-company (in cooperation with the Irish Cruising Club, the British Royal Cruising Club, and the Cruising Club of America) and for nightly entertainment ashore. About seventy-five yachts took part, coming from a dozen countries. Lasting friends were made, not the least of which was the ancient, mysterious country of Eire herself. For it is easy to imagine groups of Druid pilgrims marching along, with their banners flying, across the grassy clifftops, or giant fires burning in the round towers atop each promontory. Now they, as well as the old castles, are crumbling, but play a part still as navigational aids.

One day, on this cruise, we watched an Irish bright-hulled yawl work its way out of the crowded harbor at Castletownshend, in fog and force-seven winds. She was reefed down; all aboard were in slickers. Outside, the waves would be mountainous and the headlands obscured, though the gannets would still be flying, in twos and threes, low over the wavetops. A few other British boats followed later. Finally, when things lifted a bit, so we could at least sense the lay of the land, we also left.

The bright-hulled yawl was called *Cuilaun of Kinsale,* and owned by Ian O'Flaherty. She had an all-male crew–not unusual for British (or Irish) boats, though England can boast of several famous single-handed transatlantic and circumnavigating lady sailors. *Cuilaun* was about to embark upon a long trip "around the block" (from Ireland down to Antigua, up to Marblehead, and back to Ireland). Strangely, we were to meet her again in Antigua (in 1979), then in the Virgin Islands, and later in Maine. After that, we did not see her again until we met in Antigua in 1983.

Aboard her were sailors who enjoyed sailing a good boat. She was fifty-five feet, had a modern rig, and was fast. She flew a huge Irish flag from the top of her mizzenmast, and always looked shipshape, as did her crew. The parties given aboard, or sometimes in a rented dining room ashore, were a credit to the reputation of Paddy's whiskey and an Irish leg of lamb.

The planner and cook for this entertainment was a short, dark-haired Irish lad called (of course) Mike. He never stopped talking, all of it in a fey humor upon which the others punned exhaustively. This was amusing all right, but sometimes difficult when conducting a conversation. We had them all aboard for drinks on Christmas Day in Antigua, and, as I had done a piece on cruising in Ireland for *Yachting* which they liked, we were presented with a large bottle of their precious Paddy's Irish whiskey.

They told this story about Paddy's: There was an ancient Irishman who came into the pub each day and ordered a glass of Paddy's "neat," and then drank it down with his eyes shut.

"Why do you keep your eyes shut, Pat?" he was asked.

"But if I open my eyes," he said, "and see the Paddy's there, my mouth would start watering. It would thin it down."

Cuilaun's crew could not sail all the time, though, as each one had some sort of mundane job back in Ireland. They took their "flings at sea," after which they planned to settle down—for a while. Then, back to sea for another long-distance sailing journey. As O'Flaherty could not be aboard as much as the others, he had crew meetings ashore where strict accounts and navigation plans were decided upon.

In many quiet harbors between Schull and the Royal Cork Yacht Club in Crosshaven, we met other northern travelers, including a few from Sweden. Aboard the Swedish boats, the crew was by no means all male, but, rather, exhibited the pulchritude of Sweden in skimpiest of bikinis (as long as the sun shone). On one Scottish "home afloat," an older, beautifully maintained motor sailer anchored in lovely Glandore harbor, a fresh bunch of Scotch thistles was tied on the bow each morning. On another boat, a big, red sloop, were an Irish writer and his young wife, who were spending a few years tracking down and writing about local, age-old Irish myths and legends. In Castle Haven (one of its names) we found that knowledgeable sailors stopped off at Mary Ann's Pub, where dinner was served outside under the grape arbor, by candlelight. Afterward, all the clientele congregated in the bar for darts and other competitions. Next morning, I was scanning the harbor with binoculars when I spotted something pink moving along the shore. Closer inspection revealed a portly, white-maned gentleman doing exercises and cavorting about the beach without a stitch on. After a quick dip and a vigorous towel rub, he marched off in the direction of a small building.

The Royal Cork Yacht Club at Crosshaven (on the west side of the entrance to Cork Harbour) is a crossroad for sailors in these waters—sailors of all descriptions. There was Larry White, an officer of the Cruising Club of America, on his blue yawl, *Witchery*. Then there was the bearded crew of two on the twenty-five foot *Arvin* who, with quite marginal equipment, took thirty-eight days to cross the Atlantic. And there were Belgians, Germans, French, and traveling Britishers all passing through.

Quite a few foreign owners leave their boats in the care of the excellent yard for the winter, where they can be stored either in the water or "on the hard." The owners resume their voyaging over the summer. (Long-distance sailing usually assumes, of course, *constant* living aboard, without regular breaks back to civilization.)

But one pair planning to leave their boat here for the winter did indeed qualify as LDS's.

We had noticed a white ketch called *Nanook*. She was from Resolute Bay, Northwest Territories, and had a blue Eskimo drawing of an arctic bird on her wind vane. There were just two aboard her—young, dressed in woolen caps and heavy sweaters, even though it was summertime in Ireland. The girl had pink cheeks and large dark blue eyes, her husband a small beard and the lean watchfulness and calm of the pioneer.

Because they appeared to be living on their boat, as we were, we approached them. This we were to do many times during our years of sailing in European, Caribbean, and American waters.

Why were *they* out there, we always wondered. Where were they going? Where had they been? What were they like? And some of them we were to come upon again and again, so that, finally, it seemed as though we had become part of a family. This new family lived similarly in a new way, yet each member had his own individual approach.

These two were Katey and Maurice Cloughley, she Scottish, he Australian. They had met in England and gone together to teach children in the Territories, just for an "experience." But they had stayed for twenty years, getting used to three months of total darkness and the remoteness and bone-chilling cold of the north. They felt they were doing something useful there, they said.

"Ach, the darkness is not so bad," Katey said, "but it's thrilling when the light comes bit by bit again. In winter, one must be sure to keep a regular schedule, though."

"We find teaching fresh minds, uninfluenced by television and the consumer lifestyle, more rewarding," Maurice told us.

They had spent a year or two in the Mediterranean looking at the "cradle of culture" countries, and were now about to put their boat out to pasture in Ireland. They would return to the Northwest again, but perhaps just for the winter. Sailing, to them, was not only an inexpensive means of exploring the world, but was, like their experience in the Territories, a way of life that was independent and exhilarating. Their goal was to circumnavigate the globe, in stages. We would learn later how far they got.

We questioned them, on the basis of their experiences, about our own plans—as LDS sailors are apt to do whenever they meet another sailor who has already "been there." We had planned, for instance, to sail down through the French rivers and canals to the Mediterranean, and sail all winter in the "warm" Med.

"Ach, no," Katey said in her Scots burr. "You cannot do that. The Med is too stormy and too cold in winter."

"Get south as quickly as you can and spend the winter in a warm place like Tunis," Maurice told us. We had planned to stay in Taormina in Sicily, but they described the rough seas and cold gregale winds they had met there, and advised going farther south. We would have to hurry along then; we would have at least a thousand miles to go.

A Belgian group who tied alongside us at the yacht club (in a wide, red racing machine) also had advice for us, and we found we had mutual friends in Brussels. Over drinks in the cockpit, they told us which of the anchorages east of us were the good ones and where the dangerous shoals were. They gave us a tide-table book as well. They also told us that most Europeans cross the English Channel at night, in order to navigate by the lights and, perhaps, have calmer seas. They also, very thoughtfully, walked quietly across our bow whenever they had to cross our boat to reach the dock, rather than through the cockpit.

When we left at dawn next morning, we hardly recognized the docks. They were six deep in tall-masted one-tonner racing yachts from France, which had all come ghosting in during the night for a race that day.

Going eastward, we turned into Dunmore East (as the Belgians had advised us to do), at the base of Waterford Bay. Some jolly sailors had just finished a race there, and called out, "Welcome, America," as we entered. We were to recall this cordiality rather wistfully in the anti-American countries of the Mediterranean.

Again, in Wicklow, when we anchored close inside the stone breakwater, a motorboat put out from the yacht club. Its crew warned us that the harbor dried out there, and guided us to a safe anchorage. Afterward we had drinks all around.

Crossing the Irish Sea to Wales, we had a job to do for Wood's Hole Oceanographic Institution. (Many LDS sailors are asked to bring back samples of shellfish, strange frogs, pieces of rock, all kinds of things, to laboratories needing special specimens from some special part of the world.) We made numerous plankton tows, carefully recording their exact position by LORAN, and bottled them in preservative reagents. Back at Wood's Hole, they would be examined for radionuclides. The doctors there wanted to know where the radioactive wastes being released from Windscale nuclear station were traveling through the seas. Were they being taken up by plankton and other biota? Unfortunately, although they had asked us to take samples in the Atlantic as well, we were battling a gale at the specific location they requested, and were not able to take them.

The Welsh are no less intrepid than the Irish. We anchored behind St. Tudwal's Island in the north end of Caernarvon Bay one night. In the morning thirty percent of the boats we anchored among were lying over on their sides–ours included–aground. There was a forty-foot tide, so everyone simply waited calmly for it to rush back in. We were the lone American boat there. The others, in spite of a forty-knot wind, were participating in a weekend race around some buoys, while we stayed at anchor.

"This is good weather for England," one of the skippers called gaily to us. After all, it was not raining.

In our first port in England, we were met by gold braid, formality, and a large notebook. It was in Penzance, a fishing port. Yachts were tied four deep outside the tall, working fishing craft along the wharf. This meant–if one wanted fuel–carrying heavy fuel cans across yachts, up and across the fishing boat decks, past their rigging and around baskets of nets with fishhooks around the edge, on up the quay and down to the very end, then back again. The fishing boat captains were, in the main, not too patient with yachts, and they treated them rather like annoying flies. Of course, this united the yachtsmen in friendly cooperation.

The two customs officials had no trouble in locating us. They settled down in the cockpit and greeted us with stiff semismiles.

"Any Pakistanis aboard?" was their first question.

We laughed, but they were serious. Pakistanis were being smuggled in at that time for one thousand pounds a head. The smaller of the two men tiptoed about the boat, looking here and there, while the chief took down the official information. They rose, nodded, and advised us to be sure to "check in with authorities" before we left England.

We found the jolly family aboard our next-door boat giggling and tendering an invitation for drinks. This family from Bristol included three adults, two children, a dog, and a cat. The small boat they were traveling on was not particularly neat. Nevertheless, these good-hearted people, the Warrens, welcomed us to England and immediately advised us how to negotiate the English Channel coast.

"Most important, do not cut short around Portland Bill. People are apt to cut inside the buoys—or possibly can't see them in the fog. But stay out. It's shoal, and the currents toward the Bill are strong."

Pressed onward by the warnings of the Cloughleys, we could not tarry longer than a few days to visit my family in various parts of England, by rented car. (Some had been admirals in the British Navy, one had been lost at Dunkirk, all were still bound by the traditions of the Army, Navy, or the Foreign Service.) We hurried on to Cowes on Isle of Wight, one of the leading sailing capitals of the world. As we entered the Solent, a banded pigeon landed on the deck for a short rest. He was very tame and drank water from a dish and took bread from my hand before nestling his neck in his shoulder and dropping off to sleep.

Boats from all over the world which had raced for the Admiral's Cup (including the Fastnet Race) were still decommissioning at Cowes, but they had to hurry as the 1977 Round the World Race was due to start. Several World Race boats were already fitting out and having last-minute work done in the yard. Last on the list for dock space were cruising boats like us. After we were finally assigned a temporary slip, I noticed a small yellow buoy off our stern. As it turned in the tide, I read "Sewer Buoy."

Across the dock from us was a dignified couple in a thirty-eight-foot Swan. He was Admiral (retired) Morrison, seventy years old, and he had two metal hips. Even so, he still raced his boat successfully, with a crew of young men. Although the Morrisons' cruising was necessarily (though only somewhat) curtailed now, they kindly considered our plans for a two-year cruise quite adventurous, and offered hospitality and advice. They took us to the Royal Yacht Squadron of Cowes, which is in a castle originally built for Henry VIII, to watch some Sunday races. We, in turn, invited them aboard for a "formal" dinner of several courses, with candles and a fire in our little fireplace. We finished with coffee, liqueur, and fine conversation about mutual friends and experiences. Outside, it was teeming rain.

For another dinner party in England's rain, we had Group Captain of the RAF Charles Nance and his family. Most of the conversation concerned their friend, the late Uffa Fox, Cowes's most distinguished resident (outside Queen Victoria). Most sailors are acquainted with the boats he designed, but do not know that he was also a horseman and that he had four wives (the last made him live in her native France part of the year, if she were to live in Cowes). He also loved to entertain royalty and designed boats for them. He designed a boat for Nance's parents, which was to be their honeymoon boat, but when he saw that it was (characteristically) not going to be finished in time, he tried to persuade them that honeymooning in a small boat would simply not be appropriate. When they found out the truth, that the boat was not finished, they decided to go anyway—with, understandably, rather frustrating results.

One of the Argentinians (there were several South American Admiral's Cup boats in the process of being decommissioned, their crews yelling back and forth in loud Spanish) came aboard one evening. We conversed with him in a mixture of French, Italian, and German. He told us how he had been working hard every night on a boat model for his son while he was there alone, preparing the boat for shipment back to Argentina. But early next morning, we saw a pair of lady's shoes sitting neatly on the dock at the end of his gangplank, and they stayed there until nearly noon.

Most of the Admiral's Cup boats had flashy paint jobs and large names along the sides—a new thing in 1977. Nance's son-in-law, Jim Pritchard, commented that, "If they can't get attention by winning, I guess they have to get it some other way."

When we left Cowes, and left the British Isles (because our slip was spoken for, we had to leave earlier than our planned departure for reaching Le Havre in the daylight next morning), it was probably fitting that we should meet typical English weather—a force-nine gale—in the Channel. Our passage across was fairly speedy, but it did not seem prudent to proceed into Le Havre's perilously buoyed channel at night in a gale. Ragged, fast-moving clouds obscured navigation lights, first with brilliant moonlight, and then with rainy darkness. For hours, we circled in big, confused seas off Cap d'Antifer light, waiting for daylight. At dawn, we followed the channel markers to Le Havre. The markers are not numbered, but are named for generals, and their lights are powered by small windmills.

At Le Havre we entered France, where we would meet entirely different sorts of boatmen – the canal people.

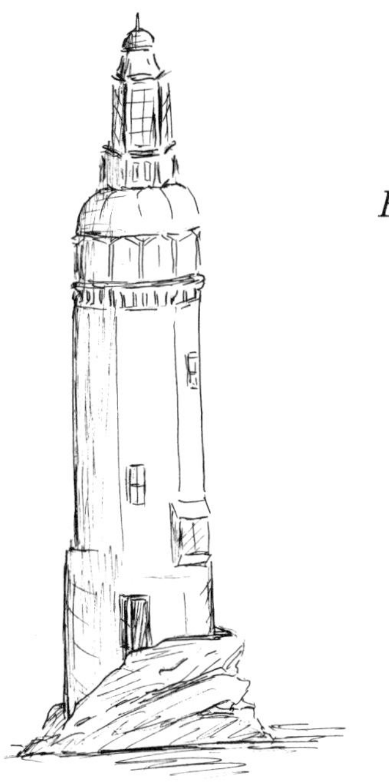

Eddystone rock

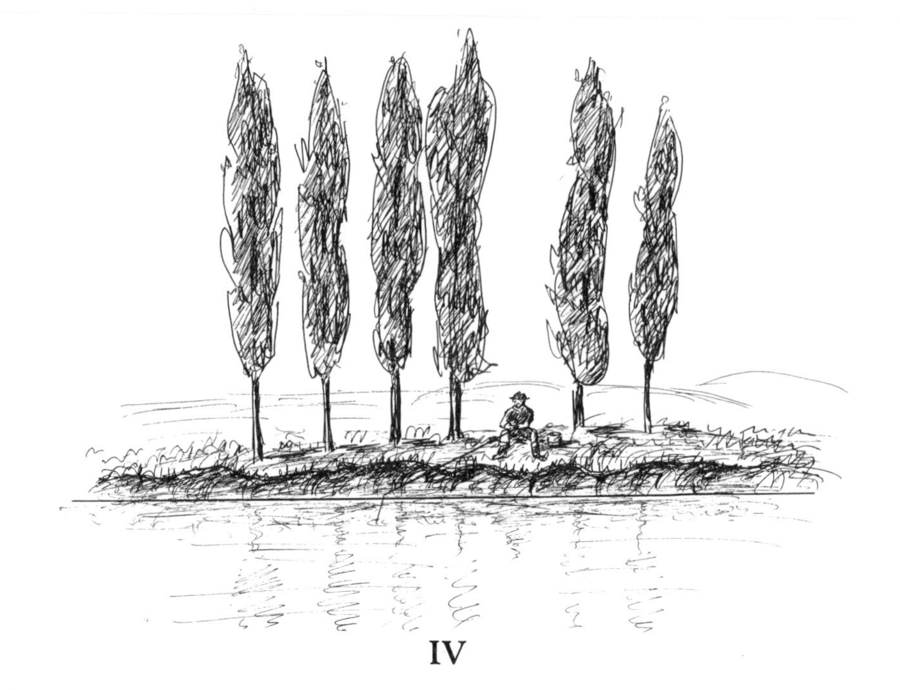

IV

Canal People

While the Atlantic and Mediterranean seas crash upon the shores of France, within her borders, a network of quiet rivers and canals wanders through her lush countryside and past her sleepy, ancient villages.

These canal networks link up with other European canals so that, with the proper boat, one can visit all the cultural centers of Europe without having to book on any trains or planes, without reserving rooms in any hotel. The best way to traverse the canals by boat is leisurely, taking time to absorb the flavor of the country (and sample its cooking) and to speak to the people about the long history of the land.

Soon this boat travel along the poplar-lined canals, in morning mists, and in company with the lusty traffic of barges and work boats, assumes the same feeling as the Impressionists' paintings—full of soft light and vibrant people—or Debussy's languid music. The boat life of the inland waterways of France is unique, and the denizens of the canals—those who have forsaken the wild seas for the warm, soft contacts of the countryside—are a very special breed. They include those who have chosen to work there, as well as those who travel for pleasure alone.

The river Seine runs down from the heart of France into the English Channel at Le Havre, and is affected by the channel tides all the way to Rouen. At certain times, at the height of the current, a dangerous tidal wave sweeps up the river, raising havoc with boats along the shores–even big ships–and causes temporary flooding. Therefore, before entering the river from the yacht basin that lies outside the Seine entrance, it is not enough to time your entry with the ingoing tide. You must try to be far up the river before peak tidal current.

Most sailboat travelers unstep their masts at Le Havre, though shipping can safely navigate up to Rouen. It is only about fifteen dollars to remove the masts (you move up in line with other boats to the crane) in the Le Havre yacht harbor, which is separate from the big ship harbor. Customs, on the other hand, is in the big ship harbor, a four-mile walk upriver.

"No, you did not need to bring your papers here," the customs officer told me in French after I had walked the distance. "We hope you will enjoy your journey through the rivers and canals of France."

However, we were to find that at every major lock on the rivers papers *were* demanded, though no fee was asked. Commercial vessels must pay, however. I would climb the slimy ladder out of the lock, race to the dock keeper's office, usually atop a tower, argue a bit with him (for his amusement, it seemed), and race back before the lock opened again.

Le Havre is a city that was eighty percent rebuilt after being bombed out in World War Two, and its new face has broad, tree-lined streets, new concrete buildings, and industrious people–a good place to reprovision and to purchase a new supply of traveler's checks. (If they are not in francs, though, many French establishments will not take them. The exchange rate fluctuates too much.)

It turned out to be an excellent place for emergency surgery also. I mashed a finger under a hatch one Sunday afternoon (my birthday) and got it X-rayed and sewed up (free of charge) by a very caring group of young doctors and nurses in the outpatient department of the hospital.

"Stop at a hospital in five days and get the stitches removed," they said. And the hospital five days away was very impressed with their work.

From Le Havre to Rouen, we shared the waterway with large ships (from every country but the United States, we noticed), barges, and a few pleasure craft. We traveled along the broad line indicated on the waterway "strip" charts. We purchased these charts from Imray, Laurie, Norie, and Wilson in Huntingdon, England, along with their book on the canals of France. They are more detailed than the U.S. East Coast inland waterway charts, and give points of interest along the way—from cathedrals to cement plants to *garages des bateaux de plaisance*—and are in several languages. We were amused to find shallow areas designated *haut fond* (high bottom). Upstream is *amont*, downstream *aval*.

Our Royal Cruising Club Folio of the Seine (with its notations from recent club members' forays) advised good and bad places to tie up for the night along the way. We had also become a member of the Touring Club de France, which entitled us to stop at Touring Club establishments (most catered to small boats only, unfortunately) and to receive instructive literature.

As we glided along with the current at about eight knots, with masts propped on deck, an awning stretched over the cockpit, and a large French courtesy flag flying from our masts' supporting beam, we became simply a barge sightseeing through the rolling countryside, past the châteaus, small towns, arching concrete bridges, and bright new industrial buildings with their extensive landscaping. We were traversing a mixture of tenth and twentieth centuries.

Our first stop for the night was between two pilings (bow and stern) in front of a grainery at Duclair. In the morning, we had our first altercation with a barge. While getting breakfast, suddenly a dark shadow crossed in front of the galley window. We looked out and saw the flat, steel sides of a barge (they are around ninety feet long, and eight or nine feet to the deck, when empty). People on board were laconically tossing lines around the same piles we were using. Children stood looking down at us while chewing on some French bread. A yacht fender meant little against this huge steel monster.

"You are too big," or something similar, we called, in French. "You'll ruin us."

"We're only staying for breakfast—just an hour. You'll be all right."

Then another barge joined up, and another. We were being shoved aground. Meanwhile, jolly exchanges passed between the three barges, and lines flew about. We pointed out, in our best panic voice, that we were going aground. A new discussion ensued.

"We're going. Not enough water for us. Good day." The children waved and off they went, the barge captains jockeying the big grotesque things about as if they were small runabouts.

Generally, all our contacts with barges and barge people were not only pleasant but fascinating – though some people, as we shall see, were not so fortunate. One rule we kept was to let the barges into each lock first. After all, they were paying fees to use the locks and we were not.

These barges are self-propelled, and the family lives aboard in a spacious cabin aft, below the pilot house. Forward are often refrigeration units or washers and driers. In the center is the large hold where everything from oil, grain, sand, lumber, and machines to animals is carried. The big diesel engines are forward of the wheelhouse. For the family's comfort, a small car is carried on deck, and often there is a penned-in play yard for the children, or even a chicken coop for chickens, goats, or pigs. Each barge (or *pêniche*), has its dog. The ladies of the barges, despite their laundry and deck-swabbing tasks, are true *ladies*. They are never seen in slacks. They always wear dresses and shoes with heels, even when hauling in buckets of water from the river.

When empty, the barges look tall and formidable, each with bright distinguishing designs on its bow. When loaded down, only the tip of the bow, and what appear as eyebrows, show. There is only a foot or so of freeboard in the center. The wheelhouse aft has a raised view of the whole barge. Sometimes, barges tie together. We often saw four together with a load of two hundred bright, new Renault automobiles. Others become pushers, with unpropelled barges in front of them. The government of France is financing the development of barge transportation and is steadily improving the canal system.

Conflans, where the Oise joins the Seine, just above Paris, is the spawning ground (and center of government) for the *pêniches*. They lie six deep along miles of shoreline, along both rivers. Children can go to school here, and hauling assignments are handed out here. This is where all official barge business is transacted. The barge people are a closely knit family, protect one another, and plan entertainment and group activities for themselves. There are even barge "stores" that travel on the rivers, selling groceries and fuel for the convenience of the barges.

Nevertheless, individual barge families are cordial and helpful to outsiders (like yachtsmen) who are new to canal life. At Sens, below Paris, we were invited aboard a working barge that was parked along the waterfront because it was Sunday. No locks are operated on Sunday. We toured the huge engine room and bow facilities and the spacious living quarters kept neat and femininely decorated by "Mrs. Barge." We noticed shoes lined up outside the door on deck, to protect the family's rooms from oil and dirt from the barge.

Later, the captain and his wife visited us, and we felt they must think a yacht rather like slum quarters compared to their house afloat. But the captain *was* impressed that we had crossed the Atlantic "in that small boat"; he had never left the river canal system.

"You couldn't have really enjoyed that terrible trip." And he made the motions of high waves (like most barge people, he did not speak English). "I'll stay here in the river."

Several times, we tied to a barge overnight, leaving with a friendly greeting from the family in the morning. And once, the barge *Aurora*, whom we had met earlier, actually tooted a welcome when we met again. A friend, however, tied up to a barge that was dark and quiet and apparently abandoned, only to be awakened at eleven at night by loud music that continued until daybreak. It turned out to be a moored nightclub.

We met our first "pleasure boat" people at Rouen—Derek and Marie Littlejohn. We had both stopped at the Villiatard Pontoon for fuel and water and planned to stay overnight (as advised by the R.C.C. Folio). Derek was from London, Marie from Australia, and it was a second marriage for both. Starting with my family in England, we found, as usual, mutual acquaintances and similar interests (in engineering and aviation). They—in their well-kept, moderately sized British powerboat—were no newcomers to the canal system. And these particular canal visitors were a little different from most of the crews of the sailboats-turned-barges. Instead of working-boat clothes—baggy slacks and stretched turtlenecks—they wore clean and tidy yachting clothes. But though well-traveled worldwide, they had chosen, out of a wide selection of nautical possibilities, canal voyaging above the rest.

We spent several days touring Rouen together. We visited the oldest restaurant in France, the beautiful, bombed-out, but repaired Gothic cathedral, the winding stone streets and ancient buildings and standing clocks, and all the places "where Joan of Arc has walked." (Not one of us could remember whether the French or the British had been responsible for burning her at the stake.) Much later, we met the Littlejohns again at a little byway off the

Seine at Donnemont. We had been attracted to it because of the boats docked at a bright, cheerful outdoor restaurant. We greeted one another like old friends, had wine together, and took pictures, but we never saw them again. We expect, though, that they are still plying the canals each summer.

"Take this book," they offered, as we left them. "It'll give you more background on the countryside. Just mail it back later."

Meeting and losing friends along a long-distance yacht voyage is not much different from one's tenuous contacts along the whole journey of life. Some of them you meet again, unreasonably and unexpectedly. Some you often think of but never see, and many pass by, easily forgotten. The only difference is that, in these encounters, probably because of similar frightening and humbling experiences, friends are made more quickly, and the usual artificial walls of status or class no longer apply.

A different sort of canal voyager (though they would have had similar tastes) were the Dixon Downeys. As we were attempting to tie up at the Touring Club de France mole along the Seine in Paris (at the Place de la Concorde, no less), a pleasant man on the stern of a trim barge that had been converted to a yacht (*Mon Reve*) advised us that the traffic of barges and sightseeing boats along the river made it turbulent along the mole, and to watch out for it. Rather than tie next to the rough concrete, then, we moored to an empty powerboat ahead of *Mon Reve*. (This would mean climbing up and over its deck to get ashore.)

The Downeys had been traveling the canals for nine years. Dixon had sold his plastic-pipe company and retired. Virginia ran their several houses, including one on an island in the Bahamas and another on an island off Mystic, Connecticut. The entire interior of the steel barge, built in Holland, was now a beautifully appointed apartment. Only its slight motion in the Seine turbulence and the chuckling of the waves along its sides hinted that it was a boat. In this craft, they, and their family and friends, had visited almost every country of Europe, solely by canal. They were able to join the association of the *péniches*, and enter the locks and dockages comfortably with them.

"It's a different kind of exploring," they said, "and there are still parts of Europe we haven't seen, but can get to now–Luxembourg, Hungary, and even Russia." The next time we were to see them, though, was in the Bahamas (though not on the barge), several years later.

For only a few dollars a night, yachts could tie up to the Touring

Club mole in the center of Paris, hard by the government centers and art museums—and where apartments sell for a million dollars. At dusk, the lights of the surrounding buildings reflect in the river, the crowded modernistic sightseeing boats pass up and down, and the evening star sets behind the Eiffel Tower to the west. The club has its offices and members' showers on a floating barge (showering in rough waters is apt to make you seasick). On another barge is a restaurant. Telephones can be installed on your boat. But, although you are encouraged to enjoy yourself, you are also encouraged to move on quickly.

Yachts are docked here two and three deep, usually, and, of course, likely to meet again many times in the passage down to Marseille. It was here that we first met *Far Horizons*.

She was a white sloop from San Francisco, about forty-two feet long, with several rub marks along her hull—from an encounter in a lock, we guessed. Aboard her were a bearded man, apparently in his early forties, his blond wife, and two small children. The MacGregor family. They were circling about, avoiding the sightseeing boats and barges in the river, looking for a place to tie up.

"We're just leaving," we called to them. As we moved out into the Seine, the man asked us rather vaguely, "Which way are you going? Canal Nivernais or Bourgogne?"

"Bourgogne."

"I draw six feet," he said. "I don't know which I'll take."

We started up the Seine in company with a small red Danish boat and an American one. (The latter's skipper passed along some important instructions we would need later when we negotiated the two-mile-long tunnel at the summit of the Canal de Bourgogne.) We were now protected by ten old tires hung from the rail (purchased, by taxi, from several Paris garages) and were now a far cry from being a yacht in Corinthian condition. We motored past Notre Dame in sparkling sunshine, left France's ancient city of art and learning, and proceeded down between the poplars to the canal country.

"One hundred kilometers south it will be warm again," we were told, for it was late September and the yellow poplar leaves were falling into the canal, surfacing it with gold and warning us that winter was coming and we should hurry on.

But the canals that connect the Seine with the Rhone do not encourage speed. They wander through the countryside still attuned to the fifteenth century. Smoke curls lazily from stone farmhouse chimneys. Little villages (where shutters are closed tight by nine at night) nestle around the tall, venerable church spire whose bells ring the quarter hour of each day. And above them, on the hilltops, are the castles.

The lock keepers are retired civil servants rewarded with this job and the small house that goes with it. Usually, the civil servant promptly gets another job and leaves the lock keeping to the (sometimes aged) wife. This means the crew of a boat must do part or sometimes all of the lock-keeping duties themselves. If the keeper is cheerful and helpful, though, a coin is tossed to her in appreciation.

"Merci, madame," they answered.

Sometimes a lock keeper is obviously annoyed by the presence of yet another yacht to lock through, and either does not help or lets the water roar in all at once, instead of gradually, so the crew has all it can do to hold the boat steady in the center. At other times, angry dogs bite at the heels of crew running from the ladder out of the damp, cold lock to loop the line from the boat around a bollard up top. It is advisable to have a young, lithe crew aboard for these duties. Our Peter Huffman from Ohio was literally able to run up the wall of the lock, though we preferred that he use the ladder.

Most of the lock-keeper houses are well-kept, sitting amid flower beds and vegetable gardens (whose produce is often sold to boats) and cheerful children. Besides vegetables, fresh water is sold at many locks, but it must be lugged in containers to the boat. Other houses are dreary and bare, and work is done begrudgingly.

Climbing, as one does on the Canal de Bourgogne, to fifteen hundred feet above the start, it is possible, in some places, to stand on the rim of the lock and see the locks lower down along the winding canal, and those above, still to be negotiated. Our system of locking was as follows: we entered the clammy lock and went slowly by the ladder to let Peter shoot up with the stern line; Peter looped that around the bollard, and passed the end to me; then, he ran to receive the bow line from Bill, which he tied; either he or Bill then cranked the rear gate closed. The keeper let in the water, and Peter cranked the front gate open and jumped back on the boat. We passed out into the sunshine. The most we ever did in one day was twenty-eight locks.

At the peak of the climb, at Pouilly-en-Auxois, comes the tunnel. Here, at last, officials extract a fee, and judge whether the boat is capable of passing through. It cannot be too deep (less than six feet) nor too high (less than nine feet) and, unless it has engine enough or is small enough not to get stuck, it must be towed through (most barges are towed).

While all this consideration was in progress, we visited other craft waiting for clearance. One was a large green charter barge called *Duc de Bourgogne*, typical of many others. This jolly group of charterers was preparing to have a candlelight luncheon inside the tunnel (which is unlighted for its entire two-mile length). The crew were unfastening the deckhouse in preparation for folding it up, as it was too high to go through. In addition, the water had to be lowered inside as well. If we were not cleared to go through ahead of them, it would be too shallow for us.

The charter barge had an accompanying bus which took the charterers for sightseeing trips inland and carried extra stores. Each member of the group was assigned his own bicycle (one lent us his for a quick trip to the bakery). The barge went down to Dijon and then returned again to the start of the canal with a new group of charterers. This routine continued from early spring to late fall, year after year.

"Your request for tunnel passage is approved, if you can get through by thirteen hundred hours. The water level will be lowered at that time."

As we started in, the canal narrowed, and we passed under the wires (live and sparking) that led into the tunnel and powered the tow. When we entered, I lay on the bow, flashlight in hand, ready to shine it on a mirror tied to the bow pulpit. This light Bill would then line up with the tiny, faraway "light at the end of the tunnel." In the pitch-black darkness, that would be all that would keep us going straight. (This method was the advice given us by the American skipper in Paris.) Peter had a flashlight to shine on the side wall. It grew colder and colder and damper and damper inside. Having no reference points, we fought feelings of vertigo. From time to time, the roof of the tunnel dripped water on us and wafts of cold air came through openings in it. No one spoke.

"How old is this tunnel," I wondered. "Is that roof ready to give way?"

We scraped the side once and lined up again with the tiny light at the end. We kept on, and on, for forty-five minutes. Finally, the light appeared to grow larger, and I could see the archway reflected in the water. Then, suddenly, we were outside in the sunlight again, and starting downward, to Dijon.

"Once is enough through that tunnel," Peter said.

All along the canal we had seen fishermen solemnly sitting with long fishing poles, apparently fishing, though no catch was ever seen. We had waved and smiled, but finally were told what the fishermen thought of *us*.

"C'est votre bateau qui chasse tous les pêches du canal. Diables americaines! Tous les pêcheurs de France ne mange pas ce soir a cause de votre bateau...." And so it was our fault the fishermen of France would not eat fish that night.

Orange Filefish

We were beginning to realize how dependent the visiting boats were upon the kindness of the people living along the canals. In just little things like helping a boat tie up to the shore at night, or thoughtfully bringing a wide plank to act as a gangplank. Or supplying fresh food and milk. One Sunday, when locks were closed, we walked into a nearby village to find a taxi that would take us to see the small, ancient feudal village of Mont St. Jean. Since there was no taxi, one of the townspeople drove us there in his diesel Mercedes. (On the way, we saw a weathered white cross on a hilltop which was dated 1312.) Later, he brought his wife aboard for wine and cheese, and invited us to visit them in Dijon, where they now lived and worked in preference to their parents' home in this rural and historic area.

Below Dijon, another driver took us to Beaune to visit the vineyard country of Burgundy and the hospice there. There happened to be a balloon meet that day–five beautiful striped balloons floating in the air.

In Lyons, at the start of the downhill run on the Rhone, the last lap to the Mediterranean, we met the MacGregors again. (We were still being told that it would be warmer a hundred kilometers farther on, but winter was close behind us now.)

"Look out for the rats on the quay," they called, as we tied to the bollards on the crumbling stone quay where yachts were assigned. "Put a rat shield on your lines."

They had taken the Canal du Nuvernais, with no untoward experiences, except an argument with a lock keeper who thought Jim was berating him when he was only asking if it was all right to enter the lock.

"There's an open market in the street at the top of the steps," Elsie MacGregor told us, "every morning at eight. You walk miles to a laundry, though, and there was a collision in the Rhone below Lyons, and it isn't open for traffic yet."

We saw other yachtsmen here who, like us, were reprovisioning, laundering, and renewing funds (American Express checks). We picked up mail at the Touring Club office here. A good many of the couples were unmarried and bound for a year in the Med, to explore and work. But only the MacGregors were American.

The Rhone is a heavily traveled, commercial river, into which feed canal systems from France, Germany, Holland, and Belgium. It is wide, locks are sometimes seventy feet deep, and it is swift—currents run as fast as ten knots. Sand suspended in it grinds at valves and couplings and fastenings in engines and heads and propellers. The entrepreneurs of Lyons advise hiring pilots for the journey, but wiser sailors point out that these expensive pilots are used to large vessels, not auxiliary sailboats; that they love to cut corners to show off, and are not bashful about eating and drinking up your stores. (Others, however, have had pleasant experiences.) We took no pilot, nor did the MacGregors.

The MacGregors, however, had the bad luck to run aground—hard—and were pulled off by a barge. But the barge wanted, in lieu of salvage, ten thousand francs. Jim protested: "Take my wife, take my son, take me. I don't have ten thousand francs." They finally settled, amicably, for fifty francs, a shawl, and some toys for the children.

We met a young Scottish couple also going it alone, while we waited at anchor for a lock to be repaired. (Along the Rhone, red and white wind socks at each lock indicate the wind strength and show when the mistral is blowing dangerously down from the Alps to the north.) They were going east at the bottom of the Rhone, to the Canal du Midi and the Bay of Biscay (we wondered how they would fare here in winter winds), while we were headed west into the Mediterranean.

Each lock on the Rhone has a dam beside it, where the water falls to the new level naturally. At one of the seventy-foot-deep locks, the Scots' engine quit, and the current began to take them inexorably toward the dam. Though the gate to the lock was open, we went after them and were *just* able to pull alongside and tow them back into the lock. Luckily, the lock tender waited. While we dropped down into the damp, cold depths at seventy feet, the Scot got his engine going again, but he decided to tie up to a piling just outside the lock for the night. We continued on to reach the beautiful city of Avignon in the darkness and a rising mistral. For two days the mistral kept the quays at Avignon crowded with sailors who were not too unhappy to stay awhile to sightsee and exchange experiences. And, at last, it felt warm. We had a long discussion with the marina owner, who had spent many years working and living in Ireland.

"You never feel at home in another country," he said, "no matter how long you stay, no matter how kind the people are. You never really belong, because you have no past there, no history."

After several days of rain and fog and currents too strong for us to turn and stop, of mountains and nuclear plants and the desolate Camargue, we arrived at Bayle's shipyard at Port St. Louis, at the end of the Rhone. We could easily tell where it was, as sailboats were tied up three and four deep all along the dock space—some with masts already stepped.

Far Horizons was there, getting her mast stepped, readying for the Mediterranean. Jim was helping others who were waiting their turn. His ten-year-old son made himself useful climbing masts, taking lines, reaching for tools. His wife, Elsie, had already found the nearest market.

We joined them that night in their main cabin. It was crowded with all the things necessary for a family living aboard a long while. Jim was restless, wanted to get to a warm climate right away (it was October). He planned to cut across the Med—past Corsica, past Sicily to, perhaps, Malta. He did not have all the charts. Later, he studied our sailing directions and took some notes on Sardinian harbors and Mediterranean winds. (He left the notes aboard our boat, and we had to hand them across to them when we left next day.)

Jim had spent the rest of that day with another sailor, an Italian returning from four years in Finland. This man had tied his dog (his only crew; he called him his "boat dog") at the top of the companionway while he got his mast raised. But the dog had jumped down and broken his neck. Jim had gone there to try to ease the man's grief for his dog.

His wife, Elsie, told us their *Far Horizons* had been in a terrible storm off Puerto Rico, with waves "wild and higher than houses, and the wind screamed for two days." It had been too rough for the Coast Guard to come out, and they were not sure where they were. She had prayed, she said, and believed that had been all that brought them through. She had decided then that she and the children would never again sail in a boat. Yet, there she was, soon to begin a thousand-mile open-sea voyage to Malta.

When, with masts stepped, we sailed out from Port St. Louis, a sailing vessel again at last, we realized that we had come to another crossroad. New kinds of sailors and seaborne travelers would be encountered, and we would return to the stern sailing of long passages in angry seas and violent winds, as well as treacherous shores and unknown harbors.

"The Neophytes"

V

Guests

One of the subjects Long Distance Sailing sailors talk about when they gam in harbors (over a few drinks, with a view from the cockpit of the sun setting over a strange new horizon) is "guests." This seems a good time to make a few suggestions (for hosts as well as guests) that might make life easier aboard.

Most guests have a basic misunderstanding of the fact that the LDS sailor's boat is his castle, his house, his home. He has worked out the best systems–for *his* particular boat–for running both engine and sails, and for storing and caring for his equipment, tools, and spares. He has set specific limits on the carrying of sail, the rpm of the engine, and in what weather he wants to leave a harbor or remain at anchor.

His wife (or first mate) has arranged her galley in the best working order–for her particular boat–for the way she and the captain live on that boat. She has stored her food, dishes, pots and pans and other household equipment in order, and knows all the shortcuts that work for producing meals on time–on *her* boat.

The navigator (whether the captain or the mate) has studied the area being sailed, knows weather and current patterns, has studied and marked dangers on the charts, has checked guides and electronic equipment, and kept them in working order.

It is a different situation entirely from the equal sharing of a chartered boat. And although the guest is perfectly competent and knowledgeable on his own boat, all boats are not the same. Without realizing it, a guest can overwork a pump, or heat up an engine, or, in fact, hurt himself on, say, the anchor mechanism or mainsheet winch, which are new to him. It is just more satisfactory, and safer, for the LDS owner to take care of some of these things himself.

On the other hand, the desire to help is certainly appreciated and understood, and guests should be instructed as to what is *really* helpful. In addition, a boat is really a close-quarters proposition for a group of adults who are all intelligent, knowledgeable, and aggressive, and that extra quality of tact, on both sides, can ease the tension.

But a discussion of LDS guests can become quite specific—and even amusing. Here are some of the comments we have heard.

"Four or five days is as long as I can stand some guests under foot all the time," one LDS skipper told us. "Mark Twain was right. After that, fish and guests..."

"It's gotten so I don't permit anyone in my galley. I just don't permit it," a Caribbean captain's wife remarked. "I've spent too long arranging everything. If I want help, it would be nice if they'd just come below and talk to me, or help clean up."

"Well, we had one guest that took the charts right off the chart table and up on deck, so he could see where we were going," an outraged British skipper said, "and our only chart of the Aegean Sea flew out of his hands into that sea."

"I wonder why they don't realize—even when you point out politely that charts are to be left on the chart table (except when entering a difficult harbor)—that no matter how many times the navigator has studied them, he (or she) has to continually check progress, dangers, radio beacons, and so on."

"They are there for a vacation is the problem," a wise man in Malta once pointed out. "They're just having fun, while to us it is life and death—survival—to reach, enter, and moor in a new harbor, in a new sea, and in a new country, and usually in questionable weather."

"And maybe with the engine conked out or the clew of the mainsail pulled out," added another.

"They don't realize either that they are an extra responsibility," the first man said.

"The hardest part to me," a friend from Seattle confided, "is having to be polite twenty-four hours a day."

"How about the guest who considers himself a great helmsman but can't hold the course you give him—keeps falling off so you can't clear the headland?"

"Or the one that suggests putting on more sail as the meltemi rises, and, in fact, starts doing it himself?"

"Then there is always the engine expert that points out that there's a knock there—'Probably the injectors,' he says, and he starts to try and fix it for you."

"Everyone knows the one who drinks up all the beer—'Gotta have a beer first thing,' and so on."

"Or how about the water? You lie in the bunk at night and hear that water pump going and you know either she's washing her hair—and clogging up the drain as well—or he's taking a shower, which you asked him not to do until closer to a water source."

"Then there's the sun-bathing bikini girl..."

"Well, some guests think they're either on a cruise boat where they are to be entertained, or they think they are on a charter boat where it's okay to take over the boat whenever you feel like it."

"We had one guy on board who decided to run the LORAN when he knew nothing about it, and blew it out in the middle of the Adriatic."

"Well, some good friends at home just don't know how to act on a boat. First of all, they arrive with a bunch of suitcases and lots of clothes or with food you can't fit in your limited space in the refrigerator."

"Say, why does everything always break down when guests come—just to make you look like a jerk?" a veteran of six trans-atlantic crossings asked.

"And suddenly leaks develop right over their bunks in the first rainstorm."

"Ever notice how guests are always standing in front of the cupboard you want to open, sitting on the cockpit seat your tools are under, or examining the chart just as you need it desperately to check a depth, or pointing out some strange something while you are maneuvering through a treacherous shoal?"

"It's funny how guests somehow plan it so they are with you in the interesting harbors but not on the long overnight slogs."

"But wait! There *are* guests who are really great to have aboard. Like everything, willing, laugh a lot..." the man from Malta reminded us.

Guests do not have such an easy time either. We know some people who do a lot of cruising in the Med who actually call their guests "slaves." They are given the *bad* duties, like finding the laundries and grocery stores in new towns. Not only are they expected to pay a good portion for all these services, but they are the ones who lug the laundry bags and groceries back to the boat.

And even more autocratic is another chap we know, in the Caribbean, who says, "I tell them that if they want to come down and cruise with us, it'll be up to them to pay for everything – fuel, water, food, showers, liquor. I supply the boat and the Caribbean."

Then there is the Britisher who built only two bunks in his boat – so there would never be any misunderstandings.

A guide for seagoing guests, and their hosts, might go something like this.

For Guests

1. Express your appreciation for the chance to see this part of the world on your host's wonderful boat.
2. Cut your clothing needs to a minimum (but include your own foul-weather gear) and pack them in easy-stowing canvas bags.
3. Ask for (and abide by) usual practices aboard this boat and establish just where you are to take part.
4. Assume that your hosts know you are a good sailor (or cook, or whatever) and do not feel compelled to impress him with the fact throughout the trip.
5. Remember that the boat is now a *home*, where you would not dream of helping yourself to your host's tools, rearranging the cellar, turning on the oil burner, or pointing out that the roof leaks. Nor would your wife bustle into the kitchen and take food out of the refrigerator which might have been planned for some other meal down the line. Nor would she invite other guests to the home for cocktails without consultation first.

Limpet

For Hosts

1. Tell your guests how glad you are to have them aboard and what a help it will be to you.
2. Show them where they live, where they can stow their things, what will be the best time in the morning for them to use the head.
3. Show them around the boat, including all the deck gadgets.
4. Give them a rundown of general practices aboard the boat, and tell them what they can do to help out—on deck, in the galley, and in the chores on shore.
5. Understand that guests, especially those who are sailors themselves, want to help, and give them a chance to do so without upsetting your own well-worked-out routines, or endangering themselves.
6. Show them, on the chart, where you are going and what the course is before you start off, and keep them up to date on your progress.
7. Financial arrangements are up to each individual skipper, but whatever they are, they should be spelled out right at the outset. Perhaps the best arrangement is the "kitty," where each couple puts in a few hundred dollars, and all bills are paid from it.
8. Impress upon nonsailing guests, before they arrive, that sailing is not an exact science. You may not be able to arrive at the beginning point or ending point of their cruise on the exact dates selected, though you will do your best.
9. Relax and enjoy your guests and give them a good time.

Atlantic Needlefish

Guests who tactfully and cheerfully fit into a cruising boat's regimen are so appreciated that they probably graduate into the category of Crew rather than Guest. Their memory is cherished, stories about them are many, and a berth aboard will always be ready for them.

Egyptian Felucca

Mediterranean Sea

Here is the microcosm of the world.

Here is the birthplace
(include Sumeria, Greece and Rome, Egypt and modern Europe)
of not only culture, knowledge, art and laws
but of professional, mechanized war.

Perhaps it is the conflicting climates –
the tall and frigid mountains, opposed to
the endless, frying miles of sand, surrounded by
the indifferent, unforgiving shores of rock –

that have set the stage
for battle deaths in the millions
for walled and buttressed cities always changing hands
for ideas and loyalties fomenting hatreds and attacks.

Perhaps it is just a preview for the world –
of the dangers of isolating nationalities
of the folly in funneling science into war
of the fate that follows on debating's end

that has won the appellation for this sea –
the wine-dark, blood-dark sea.

Ancient Greek Trireme

VI

Run for Shelter

All over the northern Mediterranean Sea, between October and December, small vessels—even the local fishing craft—must seek shelter before the arrival of the violent winter north winds (called the gregale in Italy, the mistral in France, meltemi in Greece, and boro boro in Yugoslavia). For winter in the Mediterranean is much different from the benign, luxurious warmth of the Caribbean.

Landlocked, ringed with rock cliffs, bordered on the north by the mighty snowcapped Alps, on the south by vast, hot deserts, it is a caldron of vying weather patterns. It is when the frigid mountain air breaks through and rushes across the sea to lower pressure over the hot deserts that it is the most dangerous for the seaman. Steep, violent seas build up within minutes, and with only rock shores to crash against, the waves reverberate back upon themselves endlessly. It is no place for fishermen to be, nor for the less rugged yachtsman. And sometimes, the mistral, or the grègale, continues for days.

Many sailors new to the Med—ourselves included— have not quite believed that conditions could be that bad, and still carry pictures of a sunny Mediterranean in their minds. Without having made preparations ahead of time, then, they find they must somehow get south, forever south, until it is safe to stop for the winter.

In fact, much of the Long Distance Sailing sailor's life seems to be spent in such forced long passages–to reach a stopping place before a storm season is upon him or certain dangerous local winds begin, or to reach a provisioning or repair port, or to meet crew or guests. Although shipping out in your own boat seems like freedom itself, the demands, the slavery to schedules, continue.

Boats thus bent upon making a destination have no time for socializing in harbors where they briefly stop. Crews have been sailing since dawn–or for days at a stretch without stopping–and are interested only in filling the needs of the boat and crew and then collapsing on the bunk for a few hours before they press on again. Any encounters will be made to exchange information–about weather broadcasts, harbors to avoid, friends not recently seen–or they may involve less pleasant altercations, like anchoring tangles, collisions, or even thefts.

The boats leaving Port St. Louis at the end of the Rhone, then, would be embarking on "Operation South," though each would have planned his own expedition differently. Jim MacGregor planned to go direct, without stopping, with his little family, all the way to Malta. The Italian would wait for his wife to join him and sail slowly, and sadly, along the Riviera to Genoa.

Others would sail westward to a Spanish port like Majorca or Jose Banus. Others would go south to Italian ports like Ischia, or to Malta or to Tunis. We–until we met the Petersons on *China Clipper*–were still considering some Sicilian port. (We had eliminated the Cloughleys' suggestion of Tunis, as we'd found that in the winter of 1977 Tunisian ports were sometimes closed to yachts.) At any rate, we would not call at Marseille.

"It's a den of thieves, truly," Frenchmen in Port St. Louis warned us. "Lay a tool on deck, turn a second to look at something, then reach back for your tool and it's gone. Go on to a marina like Pointe Rouge and take a taxi back to Marseille."

We met the Petersons, who changed our whole itinerary, in Bandol, on the French Riviera, through friends–Etienne and Elizabeth Lotthé–who lived there. Martha and Dale Peterson, an attractive couple in their thirties, lived aboard their forty-eight-foot Sparkman & Stephens sloop *China Clipper* in the port of Les Lecques. Originally from the United States, they had been sailing in the Med for several years, stopping for a year at a time while Dale took jobs ashore. A tall, dignified graduate engineer, he was now working at Comac, an international dredging and underwater construction company. When they had enough "cruising money," they would probably move on, they said, though Martha thought, now that she felt at home speaking French, she would rather like to stay there awhile longer. She, a pert and tidy brunette, had a job too, and they simply lived aboard *China Clipper* as if it were their house in France–only there would be no property taxes to pay. They took trips about the Mediterranean now, on vacations, but they had sailed the length of it (nearly three thousand miles) in all seasons, and could pass on valuable advice to us.

"You must try to make Malta for the winter. But it is already late, and you must start right away," they said.

"We had thought of somewhere in Sicily, and then planned to move on to Greece in, maybe, February."

Martha looked doubtful.

"It would be better later, about April, to start for Greece," she said.

"And Malta is better for the winter. There's a large international group of yachts there, it's not as expensive as the Riviera ports, it's warmer, and it's an interesting place," Dale said. He added, "Also, your boat will be safe there, if you want to leave it. Whereas, in Sicily, if you leave it..." and he shrugged his shoulders.

We sailed to Hyeres in company with them one weekend (taking pictures of one another's boats along the way) with the Lotthé family aboard our boat. We talked of Atlantic crossings, of the high price of insurance for such crossings (only Lloyd's of London would insure them at all), and of Dale's work with Comac. He had not meant to become so interested and involved in his work, and was not sure when they would get away again for extended cruising, or, indeed, even *if* they would.

But they kept warning us that we must be on our way south.

"Don't go all the way around by Genoa and down the Italian coast," they advised. "Go across to Corsica from Monaco, stop at Macinaggio–a small town with a safe harbor at its northern tip–and cut over to Elba. It is a beautiful island. Then go directly down to Sicily and on to Malta."

We had told them we wanted to stop and visit different ports along the way and not simply make a long passage of it, but we were to find later that it was too cold for long night passages anyway. A full day's exposure, with only two of us, was enough. And others going our way seemed to agree.

There was one exception, and a very curious one. It was also our first brush with yachting criminals.

It was the middle of November in St. Tropez, and a fifty-knot mistral had been blowing night and day for four days. Most everything was closed for the season (*fermée annuelle*), while those concerns that were open were barricaded against the mistral winds and the seas breaking over the harbor seawalls. We were tied to the quay with five lines from each corner and double anchors off the stern. Even so, we swayed and pulled and lurched constantly in the roar of wind and pound of waves against the hull.

One night, as we were eating our dinner aboard, someone knocked at the cabin window (had somehow climbed aboard).

"Do you have jumper wires? I can't start my engine."

As it happened, we did not have any. The face disappeared. We looked out and saw lights on the boat alongside–a forty-foot, strong-looking cutter–and several people on deck. They did lots of running to and fro and wandering about the deck carrying ropes and looking at the mast. They appeared to be unfamiliar with the boat.

Somehow, they got the engine started, and it remained running quite a while, as they walked about the deck. All the time, the wind was blowing around sixty knots. It was raining and pitch dark. Then, unbelievably, they began untying the lines. Suddenly, one of the girls started to crawl off the bow, but she was dragged back by another girl and one of the men. They slowly backed away from the quay and started out of the harbor, against the wind. What made it so important to leave at that hour in those conditions, we wondered. The next thing we heard was a fire siren, and then there was only the wind and the rain.

Next morning, we read in the St. Tropez newspaper that a forty-foot sailing yacht had crashed on the jetty during the night and had been completely demolished, though the people had been rescued from the jetty by the fire department. The paper asked several questions: why had the yacht gone out at night in such bad weather; why was the owner not aboard; and why had he allowed a friend to "borrow" the boat at that time? They concluded it was probably a case of barratry.

Along the Riviera coast, sailors are actually catered to. In ports like Bandol, Cannes, Villefranche, Antibes and Nice, you will see many fast racing yachts, as well as large (eighty to one hundred feet) cruising sailboats (usually flying the Panamanian or Liberian flag). And they are moored in prominent positions along the waterfront quay rather than being relegated to the "sewer area," as they are in some other countries. (Many boats winter here, in fact, though usually without their owners aboard.) Often, visiting LDS sailors find that marinas do not charge for the first night's mooring, but that fees increase each successive night.

French cruising charts show buoys and lights in large symbols, and designate from which direction of wind each harbor gives protection. Along the coasts, furthermore, are high-intensity warning lights which flash faster as the wind velocity rises. Monaco adds one thing more. On the first radio contact, the operator says, "Welcome to Monaco." As you leave, he says, "We hope you will return soon. Have a good voyage."

We left Monaco at five in the afternoon, the day before Thanksgiving. The wind was light, and, as we drew away, the lights of the Riviera were a diamond necklace across the horizon behind us. In true Mediterranean fashion, however, the wind and seas rose steadily (from the southwest) as we made our overnight run to Macinaggio. We were fortunate to have Bill and Jackie Binnian with us for the rough passage. Even when we finally rounded the tip end of Corsica, the wind still came in williwaws down the steep mountains into the harbor, but the seas were less. We tied up to a flimsy dock, and later had our Thanksgiving turkey dinner aboard.

Our first introduction to the fishermen of Italy was in Marciana Marina (not a marina, but a seaside harbor) on the north coast of tall, green Elba.

We had been sailing south all day, below Corsica's snowcapped mountains, and then turned east, to sail along the snowcapped mountains of Elba (it was like sailing through the Alps). Lights were just twinkling on here and there in this sparsely settled island when we found the dim green flashing light at the entrance of the Marciana breakwater. Inside, the small and ancient fishing village encircled the harbor, nestled below the peaks. The only yachts we could see appeared to be put up for the winter in among a spiderweb of protective lines. We tied to one of a small fleet of fishing boats inside the entrance.

The captain of the boat, the *Santa Marghereta* (Italian fishing boats are usually named after saints, possibly as a protection in the extremes of Mediterranean weather), rushed up on deck and welcomed us. I tried out a few of the Italian phrases I had been practicing, and he turned to me as though I could understand him well.

"Signora," he said. Then acting out and talking, he conveyed that he would be going out at nine unless the *tempesta* came. We could slide into the quay when he left.

An hour later, he called, "Signora, Signora."

He would not be going out, he said (acting out again). The *tempesta* was coming. He gave us some sweet coffee to drink, and we gave him a bottle of champagne. (Later, when another fishing boat, which had ventured out earlier, returned, we heard some merry-making on the quay.)

In the morning, we noticed that the captain had changed his clothes, slicked down his hair, and placed boxes along his bulwarks to make it easier for us to cross over and get to the quay. We then admired his excellent fishing boat and took pictures of them both. The wind had died, and soon we both left, after emotional good-byes.

Italian fishing boats are high bowed, sturdy, and painted white and turquoise green. Great care is given to them (they are sixty percent engine) and to their nets and gear. Although the fishing boats are seen quite far from shore, alone, often in breaking seas and dark thunderstorms, there is the same fraternity of fishermen as is found everywhere in the world. And they, perhaps even more than other "yachtsmen," understand the rigors and dangers met by sailors in these seas. They are, therefore, always helpful and cordial.

In Ercole, Italy, we saw this fraternity in action. We had come into the old, rock-rimmed harbor lying under a steep hill bespattered with villas, early in the afternoon. As we found small rowboats moored everywhere, we simply tied alongside another yacht which seemed to have no one aboard. At dusk, a fishing boat churned inside the breakwater and moored to a rowboat. Then another, and another, and, in all, nearly twenty came in, each to its own moored rowboat. Their stern lines were fastened to the quay. We were soon trapped between them. After the boats were all put away and washed down—under bright working lights and with much calling back and forth—each crew rowed ashore in his own rowboat, and the harbor was quiet again. Fortunately, we were safely out of the way, though the big, weedy stern lines hung close. At four in the morning, lights went on, engines started, and within half an hour every fishing boat had left for work.

We saw another type of Italian fisherman in Fiumicino Grande, below Rome. All along the river were small houses on stilts. Out from these houses, on long poles, were stretched seinelike fishing nets. They would be let down and then pulled up when filled. It gave the river a sort of Hong Kong appearance—like rows of sampans along the shore.

In our rush from harbor to harbor down the steep, snow-covered west coast of Italy (it seemed as though the snowline crept lower each day), we were surprised to find Anzio still involved in active sailing races (there was no anti-American feeling here now). A small group of cruising sailors had decided to winter in Ischia, but later we found it had been both cold and beset by thieves there.

As we made our tortuous way south from Naples, we only met other stragglers like ourselves, running south, in the few and far-between harbors down that long coast. The winter winds had begun. They raced down all sides of the steep mountains so that, in turning a headland, there was never a lee—only the same violent wind and short, sharp seas from another direction.

One particular French boat crossed paths with us almost every day—and unpropitiously each time. We first met her in the small, rather primitive harbor of Camerota. As we came in, she was there and hailed us. Most of the quay was taken up by local fishing boats.

"Back in here," they called, "beside us. There's room."

We dropped our anchor, European style, off from the quay, and backed down. The Frenchman reached for our stern line, and all seemed to be going well until, for some reason, he dropped the line in the water. It wound neatly around the propeller and stopped the engine cold.

Somehow we got the boat pulled in and tied up.

"I'll speak to one of the fishermen and get a diver for you, to take off the rope. I speak Italian," the Frenchman assured us.

But the fishermen were occupied with cutting up fish, weighing them, and selling them in the market until well after dark. Then they had their dinner.

"I have one who's promised to come," the Frenchman assured us again.

Finally, a brawny fellow in a wet suit wandered over, accompanied by most of his colleagues. After a little discussion, he eased into the water with his light, and we watched his bubbles move around. He reappeared.

"He needs a knife—a sharp one. He has to cut it."

A sharp knife was found. After a time, he reappeared again, holding a length of rope and the knife.

"What charge will he make?" Bill asked the Frenchman.

"No charge. But I'd give him something."

No one offered any ideas on what to give, so Bill gave him the Italian equivalent of about twenty dollars. The Frenchman was furious.

"You'll spoil them. That's too much. Now we'll all be expected to pay so much!" Everyone returned to his own boat.

At the next harbor, Cetraro, they came in after we did. We had a drink together and found they were being paid by a French travel magazine to report on the Italian sailing scene.

"Why do your research the hard way, sailing here in the wintertime?"

"Well, we wanted a little trip..."

In the morning, when we tried to leave early, we found their anchor on top of ours, so had to rouse them out. With a loud "shit," the Frenchman climbed into his dinghy, and we untangled ourselves.

Farther on, at Vibo Valentia, a poor, forgotten, dirty southern town, where graffiti on the walls were all pro-communist—and you could understand why—the French boat came in after dark and tied up near us. Their last word to us was:

"Don't tell the authorities here that you've seen us in any other Italian port." No explanation was given.

Characteristically, in the small world of LDS sailors, we saw them even later on, in the spring, in Siricusa, Sicily. They had had trouble with the boat at the island of Stromboli and spent the winter there. But they were off again—working for a different magazine now. We tied up far away from them this time, however.

A strange thing happens as one pushes, pushes on, jealously counting the miles and ports still to go. We suffered through each cold, wet, rough day, doing between forty and fifty rugged miles each one. At night, we tied up to the quay in a harbor (these harbors were too small for anchoring), sought out the supplies that were absolutely necessary (in one village, I accompanied a small boy on an eight-mile walk into the hills to a gas station to get ten gallons of diesel fuel. We pushed it back to the quay in a rickety wheelbarrow), then we fell into the bunk for a few hours of sleep after a sketchy meal.

Then, bit by bit, the boat seemed to become a third person. The three of us were racing for Malta. The three of us pushed out of the breakwater at dawn, sniffed the weather, so to speak, and plunged into the seas for another slog southward, to the next stop.

Often accompanying us were the ubiquitous *temperali*–thunderstorms–and they were included in every weather forecast. Our questions about the weather drew the response of shrugged shoulders and spread hands. The copper-colored cumulus rose to tremendous heights during the day, then darkened, dragging sheets of rain across the seas. Before its arrival, sails had to be shortened, though often the engine was not enough to provide steerageway in the squall, and a sail had to be raised again.

We had looked forward eagerly to our arrival in Messina, in Sicily. Here, we would be able to rest a few days, perhaps visit friends, before descending south again, along Sicily's shore and on to Malta–the haven. Storm winds blowing straight into the refuges along the way had precluded planned stops. Therefore, we found ourselves traversing the Strait of Messina (Scylla and Charybdis and all) and entering the harbor at night. I called on the radio, in Italian even, to ask where we should go.

"We have no time for yachts," I was told, and that was that.

We saw an open area along the big circular quay of the harbor and headed for it. A man ran out, so I held out my line toward him.

"*Non! Non!*" he cried, and waved his arms and blew a whistle. Twenty other men ran out, all holding carbines at the ready. This was the navy dock, we were told, and they pointed to the other side of the harbor.

We motored in that direction–it was raining now–and saw a few yachts, but no free spot. We put out our fenders and moved cautiously toward a big powerboat.

"*Non! Non!*" its captain cried. He said he had just had the boat painted pristine white, and the owner would be coming the next day. We were dark blue, and our fenders must have looked unclean to him. Nevertheless, he kindly took Bill along the quay until they found a boat that would allow us alongside for one night.

It was a boat with a Maltese flag, and looked like a small ark. The owners(?) were French (pleasant to return to that language), two men and a woman. The captain was dark and bearded and wore a cloak with a hood. A glimpse into the cabin showed red walls with paintings in heavy gold frames and, on the floor, lush rugs. They took our lines and helped us tie up, then disappeared inside that strange cabin. Next day, they tried to buy our charts of northern Italy. Not being able to do that, they traced them on large sheets of tracing paper. Then they left, a mystery.

Weathered in at Taormina (farther down Sicily's coast), we met another Malta-bound crew–Leo and Gigi Colfs from Belgium on their *Morning Haze*, sister ship to former Prime Minister Heath's *Morning Cloud*. The Colfs were "taking a few years off to look around," they said. (We marveled that such young couples–in their thirties–were financially able to cruise for a year or two without, apparently, having to stop, as most did, to work for a while in order to continue sailing–but many could.) Although their boat was a good sailer, the Colfs had decided it was wet and cramped for long passages, and were looking for a larger boat.

Finally, inevitably, the port is reached. It was just after noon, the day before Christmas, that we saw Malta's cream-colored buildings rise out of the sea ahead of us. As we drew nearer and began to pick out our landmarks and the entrance to Valletta harbor, we did not know that we would be making lifelong sailing friends from many different countries. For Malta is the winter mecca of Long Distance Sailing sailors.

In addition, we would find here an extraordinary history and prehistory. And we would be introduced, as well, to the politics and age-old rivalries of the Mediterranean. An understanding of these is as important as any navigational aid to a sailor lingering for long in these waters.

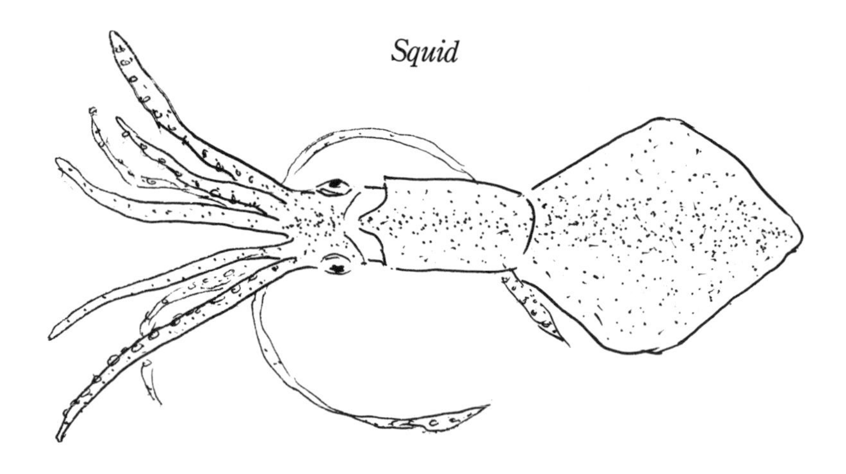

Squid

VII

Malta—Winter Oasis

Until the era of intercontinental missiles, the island of Malta – along with its smaller sister islands – was probably the most strategically placed piece of real estate in the world. The low, flat rock of only ninety-five square miles was the keyhole between the western and eastern Mediterranean, and between Christian Europe and Muslim Africa. Whoever controlled the island controlled the Mediterranean.

Over the centuries, it was taken by the Italians from Sicily, the Phoenicians, Carthaginians, Greeks, Romans, Byzantines and Muslims, the Normans and the Spanish. Finally, the Knights of St. John of Jerusalem, who were chased from Rhodes by the Turks, came to Malta. There, they successfully withstood a siege by the Turks in 1565. They built fortifications around the harbor, and up above the ramparts, the town of Valletta. After two hundred years of peace, Napoleon stepped in, but was quickly defeated by Nelson's navy in 1802. The British stayed in charge until Malta achieved her independence in 1964.

Malta has an even older history, tantalizingly hinted at in the ruins of fifth century B.C. temples – stark monoliths standing high against the sky and sea beyond – and its prehistoric cave at Ghar

Dalam containing fossils of extinct dwarf elephants and hippopotami. And it is said that Odysseus was shipwrecked on sister island, Gozo, and that he stayed for seven years with Calypso. A later shipwreck victim on Malta itself was St. Paul. In World War Two, Malta suffered bombardment night and day by Axis planes. It held them at bay with three famous old, slow biplanes called *Faith, Hope,* and *Charity,* until the British could bring in Spitfires and Hurricanes.

Now, as the Maltese jealously defend and develop their new republic – and officials of countries like Libya and China obsequiously "advise" them – the Grand Harbour of Valletta, and its many arms, provide haven from the violent Mediterranean winter winds and seas for ships and yachts alike.

When we entered the harbor, we followed the directions of the Royal Cruising Club Folio for Malta, and took up a course between the highest hotel in Sliema (the Perluna) to the west and the highest church steeple (Anglican, for the present) to the east, and passed between the forts built by the knights during the siege by the Turks. Because the Grand Harbour itself is reserved for commercial and naval vessels, we turned right, just beyond the Royal Malta Yacht Club, at Fort San Angelo, into the arm of the harbor called Marsamxett and into Lazaretto Creek. We were heading for the Manoel Island Yacht Centre. Flanking the creek, on both sides, were several hundred vessels, flying flags of every country, in all sizes and types, and moored Med fashion – stern to the quay, bows to barrels in the creek channel. As we eased into the last "slip" – the temporary guest slip – a man in western American dress took our lines.

"Welcome to Malta, Americans," he called cordially – the first American voice we had heard since leaving France.

He was Zane Mann, he told us, and he and his wife, Esther, were aboard a blue and white Mediterranean motor sailer – *Flapper II* – a few moorings away. They would be there all winter, too. He directed us to the Yacht Centre office.

Before we arrived there, however, two uniformed officials (one from customs, one from immigration) came to meet us and stepped aboard the boat. Over a drink in the cabin, they explained (it was fortunate that the Maltese spoke English as well as the impossible Maltese) the rules and regulations, and took our passports and ship's papers. The most important regulations seemed to concern selling things – like color TVs – that the Maltese could not get in

Malta. And if anything from the boat – dinghies, outboard motors – were stolen, it meant we had to pay the value of them, plus the duty, because, presumably, we had really sold them! (We put them inside for safety for a while, but it was unlivable, so we just tied them to the boat again, like everyone else.) We noticed that the officials handed out many rules and regulations and papers to sign, but no helpful advice. That we would have to get from our fellow LDS sailors, we guessed.

Next to us along the quay was a boat called *Honnalee*, flying the Canadian flag. Flush from our big six months of travel from New York to Malta, we invited the owners, Roy and Rika Gingell, aboard and asked, "How long ago did you leave Canada?"

"Well," Roy (a retiree, like ourselves) said quietly, "we really left Canada about ten years ago. We left Vancouver, sailed through the Pacific, all the islands, Indonesia, Australia, the Indian Ocean. We just came up the Red Sea into the Med this summer."

Ten years! We looked at their boat and at them. The boat looked a little tired, but not bad. And they looked fine – healthy, happy. Rika, especially, was full of enthusiasm and plans. They apparently had no terminal date for their cruising.

When we asked them to sign our ship's log, they found the Cloughleys' name there. They had seen them in the Pacific and heard their tales of the Northwest Territories. They had wondered what had become of them. And they recognized the MacGregor boat, *Far Horizons*.

"Oh, yes," Roy said. "They passed through here just before you came. But they hurried on. Everyone told them winter was no time to travel in the Med, and to stay here like the rest of us, but he wouldn't listen to anyone."

"Didn't Max say he was missing?" Rika said.

"Yes, that's right. Max – from the Australian boat down a way – has a ham radio and the hams have been trying to locate MacGregor. He was supposed to be in Alexandria weeks ago."

We were dismayed to hear that this little family was presumed lost.

"Max says the Pardeys are overdue in the Indian Ocean. They started out in the monsoon season. They were advised against it, too."

This was typical of the way LDS sailors keep track of one another – and pass on advice – in their small world. Roy and Rika had met well-known cruising couples like the New Zealand Hiscocks and the British Smeetons, as well as the Pardeys, in their travels. And they had met the Australians, Max and Shirley Vanderbent, in their red ketch *Shikama* that summer while struggling up the Red Sea to the Mediterranean.

"I never want to see the Red Sea again," Roy said. "The current and wind are against you all the way, and you are not allowed to come ashore anywhere."

"It seems as though it will never end," Rika said. "There are sharks there, too. But it was better after we joined up with the Vanderbents."

Roy and Rika had run a marina in Vancouver for about as long as they had now been cruising, and toward the ten-year mark, they began to plan a long cruise of their own. When they decided on a boat—a fiberglass forty-three-foot sloop—they sold out, shipped out, and started west. Now, their boat was decorated inside with the south sea artifacts they had picked up on their passage through the islands. They kept talking about their rough Red Sea trip, and Rika, especially, seemed rather tired by it. Roy was about to rebuild the engine as a result. So it was not surprising that later, when the northeast gregale winds began, bringing a rough surge into the harbor, they pulled out of Lazaretto Creek and found a quieter mooring in Whitehall Creek, another arm of Valletta's Grand Harbour.

One side of Lazaretto Creek is Manoel Island, the other Tax Biex, and a bridge connects them to the town of Gzira. The Tax Biex side has the grander boats—hundred-foot powerboats, flying the Panamanian or Liberian flag (one carried a car on deck), and eighty-foot sailboats (motor sailers) with captain and crew (they would be chartered for months at a time).

One of these was a large black, "Bristol-fashion" French yawl called *Marie Pierre*. Most of the winter, the crew worked aboard bringing the topsides, decks, brightwork, and wooden spars to a high gloss. Her bow anchor was farthest out in the channel, and marked by a small buoy. When the gregales came, she would be pulled out to it from the quay.

As spring approached, her crew appeared in uniform, and she was one of the first to leave. Horns blew and bells rang to wish her Godspeed. We were to see her many times—in Greece, Italy, and Spain, and, later, in the Caribbean in Gustavia Harbor, St. Barts. When she anchored, she raised a black ball on the forestay to show she was at anchor. When she got under weigh, bells rang to mark the fact that the anchor was up; the black ball came down and sails were raised. Her varnished gig for going ashore was raised on davits. Quite an inspiring sight.

The rest of us—boats ranging from sixty to twenty-five feet—were moored on the Manoel Island side. As winter settled in, we became a small village of boats, with, only now and then, a stranger entering or leaving. We got to know one another well. After all, we had all made the same decision: to leave home to see the world on our own boat. It made it easier to proceed into more personal conversations, like *why* we had made that decision. But, of course, the real fact that we were essentially strangers, meeting perhaps momentarily, loosened tongues as well.

We met the core of the "village" at a Christmas cocktail party aboard *Honeybird*, a fifty-foot steel ketch belonging to an American couple, Lou and Al Hayden. We went along with Roy and Rika. Zane and Esther were there, and the Australians, the Vanderbents, as well as a couple from Bristol, England. Everyone was in grand spirits.

The main cabin of the *Honeybird* was above the deck, with windows on three sides. We sat around a large, polished mahogany ship's table in the center. On three walls were rows of books and records and tapes. It was a cabin belonging to people who were interested in the good things of life, and read and thought. Off to one side, Al had his navigation table and radios. The galley was several steps down, aft. As we gathered, the sun was setting over the village of Gzira, at the head of Lazaretto Creek, and its light picked up the warmth of the wooden table and features of the sunburned faces collected around it.

Al was a retired architectural engineer—he designed large installations like airports all over the world—but he seemed, then, more artist than engineer. (We did not learn the full sad story of his retirement until much later.) He was slightly built, though strong, graying, and with a serious, rather lined face. Lou was dark and warmly friendly, though somewhat reserved. She designed and made jewelry. Last year, while wintering in Ischia, she had had a mild heart attack. They had been cruising in the Med for four years.

Al had found *Honeybird* in the Canary Islands, after he retired from his company in England, and planned to move aboard ship.

His boat would be his home—and the lovely *Honeybird* was just that. Her former owner had sold her because his wife had not liked boat life. Al, along with a black man and several other friends, sailed her to the Med and picked up Lou in Spain. They had moved slowly eastward since then. *Honeybird* looked a little tired now, a little rusty around the edges. But Lou and Al worked on her a little each day, and enjoyed living on her in the meantime. There was always that day ahead when she would be scraped down to bare metal and repainted.

Although we had arrived feeling rather proud of our sea passages—the transatlantic and winter Mediterranean ones especially—we were a bit behind this group. Zane and Es had spent about three years in the Caribbean (Zane had written a book on it). They had sold their Sparkman & Stephens sloop there, and bought the Mediterranean boat, *Flapper II*, in Europe. The S&S sloop was too fine for the short seas of the Med, Zane said, and he preferred the heavier, high-bowed motor sailer of Mediterranean design. They had been sailing here nearly two years. Max and Shirley Vanderbent had, after being in the boat business, designed and built their forty-five-foot molded plywood yawl, *Shikama*, and had already spent two years coming from Australia in her. The Bristol couple had sailed down from England a year ago, and their small sloop was now "on the hard" (in the shipyard) while they lived in an apartment in Gzira.

At first, we traded experiences—those hair-raising ones all sailors have—unforecast weather, broken stays, ripped sails, dead engines, nightfall and no harbor in sight, and sometimes, strange following boats or shots across the bow to warn of forbidden waters. (We spoke of a case in the East Indies where people on board a sloop were shot dead by unknown people on a supposedly uninhabited island.)

Then, as we began to feel all of a family, though we had only recently met, more personal concerns surfaced.

Es Mann told about starting down the Hudson River, destination the Caribbean. Es is a tall, attractive, and animated brunette, now perhaps a little more weathered than she would have been if they had not been sailing for four years or so (which can be said of *all* LDS ladies!).

"Suddenly I realized that if I didn't like living aboard a boat, there was no place I could go. The house was sold, everything we owned of value was aboard, and we might be on board for years. I thought, 'What has Zane done to me?'"

She had held a good job before Zane decided to retire from the investment business and Wall Street. (He had, we discovered, worked with a Long Island neighbor of ours.) Later, Es was to tell me she had to return to "the States" for a month each year to touch base with civilization – clean, feminine clothes, business talk, old friends – and before she returned to the boat she instructed Zane to "get himself cleaned up."

Both Shirley and Rika said they had been planning to retire at sea for a long time. Being in the boat business, they had carefully selected their boats and equipment with Long Distance Sailing in mind.

"While we were building our boat," Shirley, a cheerful blonde, said, "our employees and friends helped us on weekends. When we had to turn the hull right side up, so we could start work on the cabin, the whole neighborhood helped. Of course, when it was finished – finally – they all joined in the celebration for our departure. We didn't have time for any regrets."

"Well, we've been wandering around the Pacific islands for such a long time," Rika said, "it's good to be in one spot for a while. Sometimes I'm pretty tired," she added. "More this year than before, I guess. We haven't seen our children for several years, though we hear from them."

"Ten years is a long time," someone observed.

"What about you, Lou?"

"We never exactly planned this," she said quietly. "When Al lost his company in England, we didn't have much left. He's always wanted to sail in the Med, so he looked around for a boat for us to live on for a while. Well, here we are," and she smiled around at all of us, and offered us another drink or more cheese and crackers.

The men had stopped the technical talk about alternators and diodes and bleeding air out of diesel engines and were evaluating the impact of twentieth century "civilization" on the more primitive parts of the world. By now the sun had set, and we moved closer to the table in the ship's dim lights.

"When I see Coca-Cola and McDonald's in Indonesia and cowboy ranches advertised in Malta," Al said, "I really wonder about the benefits of this civilization."

"Especially," Roy said, "after you see the happy native cultures where they have their own strong moral code, where they trust and befriend strangers like us, and where they respect and protect their environment. Maybe they call on a lot of pagan gods of nature and so on, but they have a deep feeling that they must keep the plants and animals around them healthy and the water pure if they are going to thrive themselves. There they're way ahead of us."

"How about the art and architecture of sixth century B.C., the golden age of Greece?" Max said. "That perfection permeated their whole society."

"But they had slaves, didn't they?" Shirley said.

"So our claim to advancement of civilization is in social gains," Zane said.

"But somewhere we got off the track–about the time of the American Revolution maybe. After that, we grew into a country mainly focused on material improvement, material acquisition. And, finally, in the twentieth century, material worship," Al said.

"That, and sex," Zane put in.

"Going back to the social gains, though. The Civil War curbed slavery all over the world," Rika said.

"Today there is a different kind of slavery, having to do with massive concentration camps and the misuse of power," Lou pointed out.

"You know what Loren Eisley said. He looked at the gray splotches on the space view of the planet Earth, where cities were, and he said the human race might really be just a blight on the earth."

"But we human beings have the power now to destroy the whole thing, of course."

We stared into our drinks. We had lost the Christmas spirit.

"Well," said Max, cheerfully, "that's what has brought us all here, isn't it? To take a look around the world, to go back to basics, to have time to think–and talk."

"And drink. Merry Christmas, one and all," and Zane lifted his glass to the group, and the gloomy spell was broken.

Throughout the winter, each boat crew caught up on boat work. Our own schedule of work included: repair to the refrigeration and heads, new batteries, rewiring of aft cabin lights, varnishing and painting, and installing a new CW (code) filter in the ham radio. We also explored Malta and Gozo, traded paperback books, visited other boats and traded sailing "lies," took in the nightly twenty-five-cent movies (censored in this Catholic country) in the old, tile-floored government building in Gzira, and attended (as temporary members) the luncheons and evening lectures (on navigation or harbor lore of the Med) at the Royal Malta Yacht Club on Manoel

Island. The daily European *Herald-Tribune* could be bought across the bridge in Gzira, a five-cent bus ride took us into Valletta, cleaners and laundry men called at each boat, and a greengrocer (very expensive) came around each morning with fresh vegetables and fruits and live rabbits which he would kill before your eyes.

We traded paperbacks with the David Brookes, who had been in Malta during the prime days of the English government in Malta and had decided to retire there–before the Republic had been declared. They had simply liked our boat and paid a call. Aboard their *Papingo*, we were served a five-course dinner on real china, real silver, with real candles and real Oriental rugs on the cabin sole. They were using all the things they had brought out from England (in contrast to the unbreakables most sailboats had aboard). But they were finding a growing coldness toward the British in Malta. In fact, one day an editorial in the daily newspaper stated: "Never again will either the United States or the Royal British navies use Valletta Harbour as a base."

They gave us good advice for the next leg of our trip–from Malta to Greece–and we were to see them later, though for the last time, during a sudden squall in Yugoslavia.

"Especially," they warned us, "watch out for the tunny nets as much as four miles offshore, and marked at night by a confusing light on a pole."

I had hoped that they had known my uncle, Admiral Frederic Gilpin-Brown, when he had been stationed in Malta (in fact, I had looked forward to all Malta's knowing him, but no one did). They sent me on to the Humphrey Bartons on *Rose Rambler*, a tried and true sloop of under forty feet. Hum Barton–well-known in sailing circles, and founder of the British Ocean Cruising Club–had crossed the Atlantic in small boats twenty-two times! Now in his eighties, with impaired vision and some arthritis, he was limiting himself to the Mediterranean (his wife was doing the varnishing now). He was still writing for yachting publications, though, and was to win the Cruising Club of America's Blue Water Medal for outstanding "blue water" sailing that year (rather belatedly, we thought).

The cabin of *Rose Rambler* was small–Hum looked too tall for it–and crowded with books, magazines, guides, catalogues, radios, jackets, pillows... We were welcomed aboard and given articles to read and detailed advice, particularly on provisioning for the return transatlantic trip—far away at that point, but I referred to all the notes I had taken when the time came. (They did not remember Uncle Freddie either.) In spite of their vast experience, they kindly questioned us to see how we did things and what we had seen. *Rose Rambler* was on the Tax Biex side of Lazaretto Creek and a popular stop for visiting sailors from all countries.

Not all visitors to the Tax Biex side were friendly, however. One morning, a gray Maltese gunboat appeared in the harbor, manned by uniformed Maltese officials. It drew up beside one of the sleek, white, hundred-foot powerboats, and escorted her out of the harbor. (No bells or horns from the rest of the fleet for her.)

This one had been selling duty-free color TV sets to the local Maltese in St. Paul's Harbour, around the corner. Others, thus escorted later on, were accused of selling drugs. The Maltese response to these problems was simply: "Get out!" (Other Mediterranean countries, we were to observe, meted out much harsher treatment.)

Around this time, a mystery trawler came in. She tied up beside us, but her crew was oddly unfriendly. She seemed to be a converted fishing boat, the crew was mixed black and white, male and female, and the flag was constantly furled, giving no clue to her home port. We watched them doing some construction work on the boat—apparently making cupboards below. Happening to stand behind her captain at the teller's window at the local bank, I saw him deposit a tall stack of crisp, new hundred-dollar bills. The girls on board bought fresh vegetables from the greengrocer and ordered other supplies brought to the boat (liquor and other duty-free purchases could only be put on board—sealed—after the boat had been officially signed out). The girls also went singly into Valletta and bought locally made white sweaters. We watched them also practicing judo kicks on the bow deck.

It was the night before they left that a car stopped in front of the boat. In the light of the headlights, we saw one of the girls being lifted out of the car—she appeared to be either dead or completely stoned. They lowered her into their dinghy, and from there she was lifted aboard. We never saw her again. Next morning, officials gathered, papers were exchanged and signed, and mooring lines cast off.

We stood by with lines, hoping to glean some information, but all we heard was:

"We have a thousand-mile trip... Port Said, then Yemen... pretty strong wind... boat really rolls...."

The officials would tell us nothing more. Another mystery.

Malta Radio broadcast weather and traffic four times a day (usually), announcing themselves: "Hello, all ships, all ships, all ships!" Weather information was confined to a fifty-mile radius, and traffic and calls were exchanged – in English – with commercial ships in the area. (These were interesting, but sometimes crowded out the weather broadcast.) However, a good warning was given of any approaching gregale winds from the north.

Announcement of a gregale provoked frantic preparations. Besides laying in food, extra lines were put on. In fact, boats were pulled away from the quay toward the barrels in the creek, because the waves surged along the quay, making boats lurch forward and back about twenty feet. Some boats pulled away entirely and anchored off, to escape the motion. Others failed to supply enough spring in the lines – with rubber tires – so that cleats and sometimes decks were pulled loose. Gregales – normally accompanied by rain and hail, but other times by clear blue sky and alabaster-white cumulus clouds – could last from three days to ten. And sometimes boats crashed together sideways, with some damage. We experienced three of these storms during the winter.

After *Honnalee* moved to a quieter berth, a high-bowed, Turkish boat of German registry moved alongside. Her crew consisted of a blond young man and woman and a large Siamese cat. We noticed that they kept the cabin lights on most of the night, but discovered this was because Stan Mott, an American, chose to do his cartoons for *Mad* magazine at his drawing board in the quiet of the night. His German wife, Elise, a well-known dress designer, had a "sewing room" aboard and made fur-lined boat slippers (they were wonderfully soft and warm) and very small bikinis (the smaller, the more expensive). She modeled the bikinis in the spring, as soon as the sun had any warmth at all.

Then a rather old, but well-cared for gaff-rigged sloop, flying an American flag, anchored off our bow. She seemed to have only a very young girl aboard. When she rowed in one day, though, we found that her husband worked on a Libyan oil rig and was away a month at a time. His high pay allowed them to take a long summer vacation of sailing about the Mediterranean.

Toward the middle of March, while Malta blossomed out in wild flowers, boats began to disappear from the quay and reappear in the Manoel Island shipyard (excellent work is done here) for refurbishing prior to the general exodus at the beginning of April, to points east and west in the Med. Also, boats arrived from other ports–some of them from other Maltese harbors.

One of the new arrivals was a forty-two-foot Moody ketch called *Mimas*–from "May I Make A Suggestion"–with the Gillies family of seven aboard. We watched as they tied her up–with a good deal of discussion–and washed her down. Each child–they ranged from eight to eighteen, we learned later–had his own specific job to do, we could see.

"We are cruising while the children are still young enough to stay with the family," "Doc" Gillies said.

Doc owned a string of Ford dealerships back in Ontario, and he kept *Mimas* as clean as any of those cars in the show windows. Nancy was a nurse, and there was no-nonsense nutrition aboard *Mimas*. They had purchased *Mimas* in England and sailed her to Ischia, in Naples Bay, for the winter, where they had known the Haydens, the Manns, and the Colfs. They would stay to get engine parts and work done and then leave for Greece. And we would see them again and again, in the Caribbean and, finally, in the United States. Also, we would see, when we met them later in Piraeus, beautiful drawings Al Hayden of *Honeybird* did of their children, after we left Malta. He had caught the delicate essence of each child's character in very few lines.

Each morning, the officials from Manoel Island Yacht Centre, with pad and pencil in hand, made a survey of the boats still moored on both sides of Lazaretto Creek. The first day of the month, mooring, water, and electricity had to be paid for the whole month–payments for only part of a month were not even considered. In planning to leave, then, one had to be sure everything would come out even. We planned to leave from the shipyard on April first, for Greece, with a cousin from England, Anthony Wharton, along for company. (It turned out to be a day later, as my cousin's luggage arrived several flights after he did, but the officials kindly overlooked that.)

Before leaving, Max Vanderbent of *Shikama* checked over our itinerary with us, and gave us a few helpful tips.

"Don't anchor in Santa di Leuca (at Italy's heel) but go around the corner–it's not far–to Tricase. It's a small, walled harbor at the foot of a fishing village–a little gem."

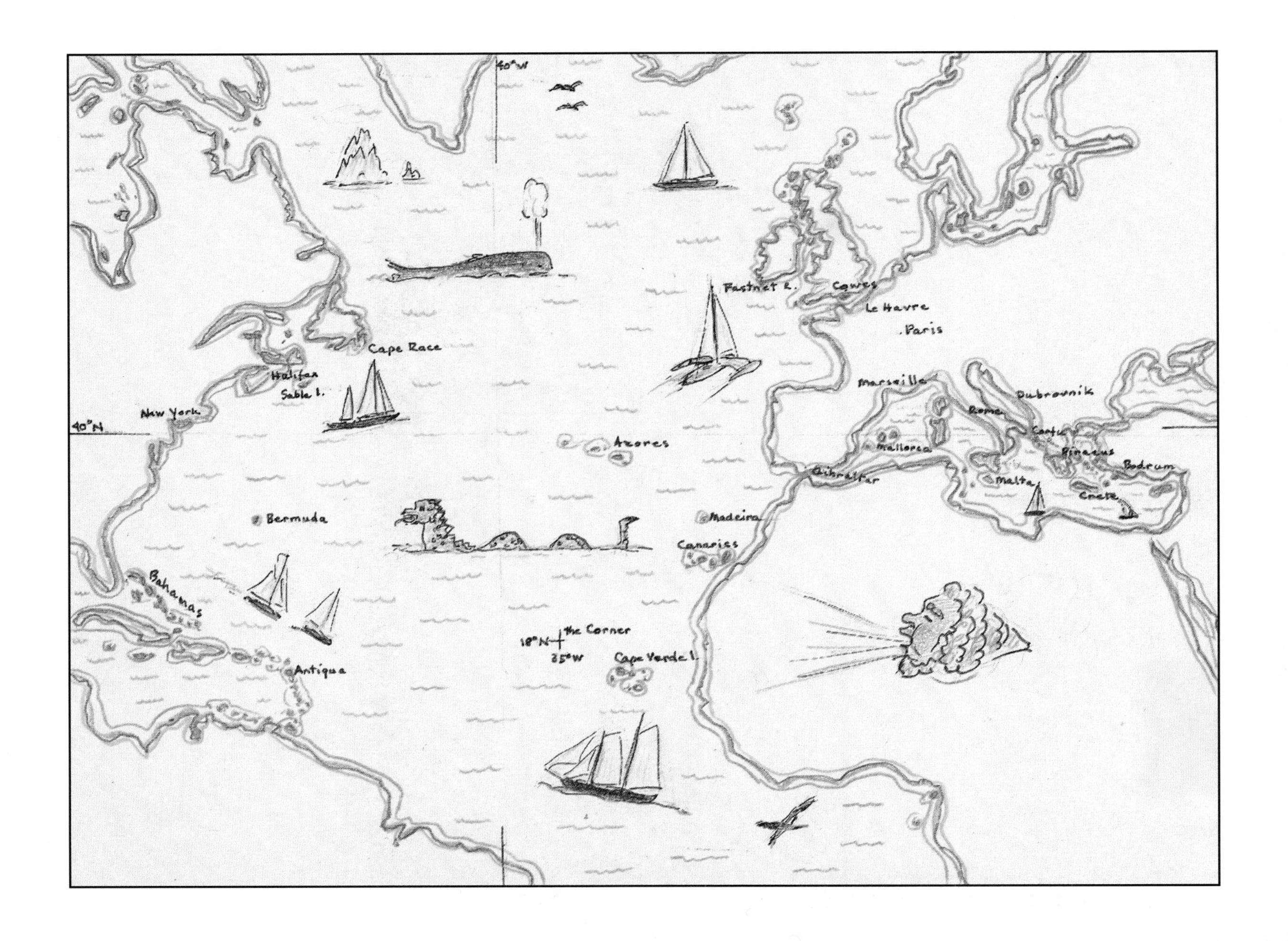

40°W
Fastnet R.
Cowes
Le Havre
.Paris
Cape Race
Halifax
Sable I.
New York
40°N
Marseille
Dubrovnik
Rome
Corfu
Mallorca
Piraeus
Bodrum
Gibraltar
Malta
Crete
Azores
Bermuda
Madeira
Canaries
Bahamas
the Corner
18°N
35°W
Cape Verde I.
Antiqua

Greek anchorage

Audacious—*the author's ocean-cruising boat, a 45-foot, shoal-draft, strip-planked yawl.*

The quiet Irish harbor at Castletownshend, County Cork.

Pastoral scene along the River Seine on the way to Paris.

Lyons' fresh produce market, open every morning but Sunday.

Sailboat race in light winds on the Saône, near Mâcon.

The friendly Les Mureaux Yacht Club on the Seine.

A typical small château along the Seine.

An elderly French cruising boat off Nice.

Taormina's harbor, lying below the ancient Sicilian town on the mountaintop.

The golden stone buildings of Valletta, above the entrance to Grand Harbour.

OPPOSITE: Busy day ashore for the fishermen in Marsaxlokk Harbour, Malta.

Unloading livestock at Mikonos, in the Aegean.

A quiet harbor along the Dalmatian coast of Yugoslavia.

The old walled city of Dubrovnik, Yugoslavia, with the Adriatic beyond.

Ubiquitous patient donkeys waiting above Lindos Harbor, Rhodes.

Audacious*'s captain and wife at Lindos, Rhodes (by E. E. Post).*

Native sailing craft in Kalymnos harbor, in the eastern Aegean.

An inland vista near Ponce, Puerto Rico.

Practicing for the Family Islands Regatta off Nassau, Bahamas.

Typical harbor where long-distance sailors congregate, Charlotte Amalie, St. Thomas.

Falmouth Harbour anchorage, Antigua.

Mimas, *moored stern-to in Malta.*

Morning Haze, *Leo and Gigi Colfs leaving Taormina's harbor.*

China Clipper, *the Petersons' 48-foot Sparkman & Stephens sloop on the French Riviera.*

Far Horizons, *coming into St. Barts with children in the rigging.*

A helicopter on the deck of the Panamanian registered 100-foot powerboat in Corfu Harbor, Greece.

Cuilaun of Kinsale *from Ireland in Peter Island harbor, the Virgin Islands.*

Rock of Gibraltar, showing the water catchment basins and the heavy levanter (east wind) cloud.

Sea Cloud*, high-class tourist cruising between the Mediterranean and the Caribbean.*

*Tied up conveniently to a restaurant near Rolleboise on the Seine (*Audacious*).*

Two hundred Renaults traveling up the Seine by barge.

Red roofs above the harbor of Charlotte Amalie, St. Thomas.

Brightly colored Maltese fishing boat—a 2,000-year-old design.

Cruising boats moored in front of a taverna, Simi Island, Greece.

A Greek boat entering the island of Ithaca's mountainous and sparsely settled harbor.

Fishing boats putting out from the harbor at Gouvion, Corfu.

Garden above Mandraki Harbor, Rhodes, Greece.

Spanish fishing boats at Motril, Costa del Sol.

Widgeon, *undergoing jib repair at lonely Acklins Island, Bahamas.*

"This island of Othonoi, west of Corfu, has an anchorage on both sides, so you can get protection from either north or south winds–you may need it."

"No, you won't be protected from winds in the Gulf of Corinth."

"You've chosen Aegean islands with a lot of history and all that, but don't miss Mikonos–it's touristy, but a lot of fun."

"It's best to go from Crete to Rhodes, rather than the other way as late as July, in the meltemi."

We set up a ham radio schedule, too, to try to keep in touch, as they were going west while we went east, but we never really made good contact, nor have we ever seen them again. (We did send a message, much later, with a boat starting off from the Caribbean to their home port of Fremantle, Australia.)

"By the way," Max added. "I heard, through a ham in Crete, that the MacGregors showed up there a week ago. I knew you'd be interested." Indeed we were, and we were to cross paths with them soon again.

We had one last sightseeing tour of Malta and Gozo with Lou and Al. We rented a car (old and rusty–a used car originally costing around one thousand dollars in Europe, cost about sixteen thousand, with the duty, in Malta). Bill drove and followed the route Al had marked in yellow in his guidebook. We had already visited the fortifications, the cathedral, and ornate buildings in Valletta, built by the Knights of St. John of Jerusalem, and we had seen the prehistoric cave with the skeletons of extinct animals. This time, we looked at the underground Hypogeum temple and the large stone ruins at Tarxien of temples to the fertility goddess–built to the shape of the goddess herself, rather like a fat, prostrate snowman of yellow Maltese stone.

After calling at the old capital, the walled city of Mdina, we stopped at the circular harbor of Marsaxlokk, where the to-be-defeated Turkish fleet anchored in 1565 but where, now, Malta's high-bowed blue and yellow fishing boats are moored. Along the quay, fish are sold, fishermen mend their nets, and laundry whips in the breeze.

We took the ferry over to the "silent" island of Gozo (in contrast to Malta's "yells, bells, and smells," as David Niven has described the British army officer's reaction to Malta). Gozo is smaller, less inhabited, more fertile, and more hilly than Malta, and the far views are longer and, indeed, more silent. We lunched at the Cornucopia restaurant (frequented by author Nicholas Monsarrat, who lived on Gozo for a time). Atop a hill, this remote stone restaurant overlooks a valley divided into fields by low stone walls, with the very blue Mediterranean beyond. An old white horse stood just beyond the restaurant wall, gazing over the valley at the same view.

We talked a little more about being "live-aboards." We were particularly curious about their thoughts, as they seemed to be prepared for this mode of living for the duration, so to speak.

"Oh no, we don't mind being called 'yachties,' even though the natives use the term derogatorily. They still take our money, after all."

"But how about the feeling of always being an outsider—just an observer, as if you're from Mars, just looking on?"

"I guess that's part of the attraction—for us. Being anonymous, with plenty of time..."

It seems that a partner of Al's had cut him out of a big contract in Iran, leaving him no alternative but to dissolve the partnership and get out. After three years of cruising in the Med, he had lost most of his bitterness, but we wondered how things would go for them—being money-short and the boat rusting beneath them, and worrying about Lou's heart. But we would keep in touch and perhaps later we would have more encouraging news of them.

Another live-aboard couple who wintered in Malta, whom we spoke to later on, had a somewhat more troubled attitude toward their continued future at sea. A British couple from Kenya, they lived aboard a large fifty-six-foot motor sailer, designed for them by Laurent Giles and built in Ireland, called *Sululu ya Pili*. She looked very rugged from the outside, but inside she was like an English cottage—broken up into white-walled "rooms," with curtains at the windows and pillows about. Like the Brookes, they, too, had their silver and china and crystal (and Siamese cat) aboard, and it was their only home.

Not that John and Dulcie Hunter were not excellent seamen. They were, and had been cruising the world for *fifteen* years when we met them. John, sixtyish, was tall and wiry, with heavy sideburns that gave the impression that he was bearded. Dulcie was younger, blond, and very energetic and intense. They had rigged their big, strong vessel for short-crew sailing—sheets led amidships, jibs were self-furling, and on the mainsail there were lazy jacks to confine it when it was dropped. A navigator's "room" in the wheelhouse was equipped with LORAN, radar, SATNAV (satellite navigation), and several long-distance radios, both AM and SSB. (I was envious.)

John had been in business in Kenya, on the coast, for about ten years when "the troubles" came, and he decided to move to South Africa. When this too appeared unsettled, he and Dulcie decided to try living aboard a sailing vessel and taking a look around the world.

"When you have been living right there—in Kenya or South Africa—it's not so easy to say which side is right," Dulcie said. "I wouldn't like to dictate. Certainly Mugabe is anxious to keep the whites with their expertise in both business and government in Zimbabwe, and Kenya's transition has been a smooth compromise."

"Dulcie's beginning to want to put some roots down now," John said. "She wants to know she has a little house somewhere. We'd rather like to emigrate to the United States, but because of quotas (we're officially Africans), we can't legally do it, and I don't want to settle there illegally, like your Cubans and so on. If some senator should take an interest, perhaps it would suddenly become easier!"

"Yes," Dulcie added, "if you had asked me two years ago how I liked my life aboard the boat, I would have been completely enthusiastic. Completely. But you ask me now, and I'm sorry, but I can't honestly say that. In a way, it worries me. Am I getting old? I'm only just fifty."

Certainly fifteen years without a break is a long time to be separated from the land. It is like flying. Flight is beautiful and exhilarating, but, finally, one needs to let down from the rarefied air into the warm earth blanket and put down once again on home ground.

When our deadline, April first, came, officials at Malta airport forecast a northwest wind, force four or five, decreasing in strength near Sicily. But lying in the bunk that night, we heard hard rain on the cabin top and a menacing roar in the wind. Because we had been inside the protective fortifications and tied to the quay so long, to me anyway, poking our bow out into the open Mediterranean on the morrow was completely uninviting. And a German boat's crew, tied next to us in the shipyard, agreed.

But early next morning, the rain had stopped, and Bill decided that the wind had slacked off enough. We untied our lines from Malta for the last time, and motored out past sleeping Valletta as the church bells were ringing the six o'clock Angelus, past the mosques and churches and balconied houses of golden stone, out through the massive bastions, and into the already choppy and windy Mediterranean.

Soon, it had all sunk down below the horizon astern. The only thing in sight was a small white triangle, presumably the tip of the sail of the German boat, and it followed, way behind, all day.

VIII

The Nitty-gritty

Just like housewives talking over the back fence, Long Distance Sailing sailors in port gossip about food prices, the best laundry, and where good engine mechanics and refrigerator repairmen can be found. Even though they have shipped out for the freedom of the seas, these problems still plague them. The only difference is that help is *not* just around the corner, and without the advice of other sailors or fluency in the language (or both) it may take a long time to find.

Food, actually, is no problem. After all, Europeans (even Asians) also eat, and sometimes the meats and vegetables in the colorful open-air markets in each town are fresher and more attractive than supermarket fare. Certainly the lively assemblage of people is more interesting, and the new foods to be bought lend a little spice to the cuisine. But here are a few food problems we did encounter: In Yugoslavia, they have not heard of queuing up—the fellow with the longest reach and loudest voice wins at the meat counter. Also, when buying, say, a leg of lamb, the head of the lamb is often thrown on the scale as well. In Gibraltar, it is unwise to buy meat the day of departure as it can be tough and uneatable, with no recourse far out at sea.

Showers are always a problem. Unless the boat has plenty of water for showers, it is best to take a hotel room for a few hours to allow the crew to shower. (Some hotels may raise eyebrows, but most allow it.) Large marinas, of course, provide showers (though there are few marinas in foreign waters). However, many of these are open shower rooms without privacy, with poor drainage and cold water. In some towns, we were sent to public showers, usually associated with sports arenas, which suggested the gas chambers. Once, we showered in a cubbyhole at the back of a marina office, another time on a rocking barge in a well-traveled river.

A coin-operated *laundromat* is a rare luxury. When they exist, in Europe, usually the proprietress insists on doing the laundry for you (and charges accordingly). In any event, it will always involve carrying the heavy bags for many blocks through town ("Go a hundred meters straight ahead, and then turn right"). In Monaco, we carried them up, up the stair-streets there, and, in Lyons, we carried them past old, decaying dockside buildings where wafts of ancient air seeped out through cracks in the walls. In some places, like Corfu, in Greece, local officials advise laundresses who smilingly return the laundry with bills for over thirty-five dollars. Then, in big marinas like Zea Marina, in Piraeus, hanging laundry to dry about the boat's lifelines is forbidden.

The problems of *mail* and *money* are common to all LDS sailors. We happened to have taken to heart the American Express advertisements, and had our mail forwarded to AmEx offices in each country. We picked up traveler's checks here as well. Others use VISA or Barclay's or MasterCards to get funds. It is helpful to get the traveler's checks in the denominations of the country's currency, so that shopkeepers do not have to worry about the exchange. We only had one mail problem—other than mail in Italy, where it always gets waylaid—and that was in Athens. We found that *Mimas* was having the same problem. The mail girl at American Express, for some reason of her own—eyesight, psychosis, meanness—refused to give out the mail, even though it was plain to see when she flipped through the pile that there was mail there. Finally, we all paid a visit to the manager, who retrieved our mail for us.

With *diesel* fuel, there is not much problem. But *alcohol* and *kerosene* are harder to find. *Propane* is more available, as Europeans do a lot of camping. They call it camping gas. *Briquettes*, for the same reason, can be bought. However, there is one difficulty with propane—the metric threads on the filler hoses. This means that, unless you make an adapter, or the gas supplier is uncharacteristically inventive, the tank can only be filled by the regional supplier (the supplier to the suppliers). He will not want to simply exchange the empty for the full tank, but will fill the tank with an adapted hose connection. In Southhampton, England, we were told that they were not allowed to sell us propane, but to leave the tank anyway. We returned, and the tank was full—no charge. In Marseille, on the other hand, we spent a full day in a rented car going "straight ahead for three hundred meters and turn right," before finding the source supplier out by the airport.

Telephoning is actually more convenient and more civilized than it can be for strangers in the United States. European telephone services are run by the governments, usually associated with the post offices. Calls are put through by the operator, and taken in a private booth. Payment is made after the call is completed. (Calls made from hotels are nearly double in price.)

There are problems with *water.* In the Mediterranean and the Caribbean, at least, it must be paid for—five or ten cents a gallon. To insure a baseline purity among the large array of town waters they take on, most LDS sailors install an activated charcoal filter that removes impurities and bacteria. (Recreational vehicles also use them.) They must be changed about every three months. We took along some tablets that could be dropped into the water to purify it, but never used them. Some LDS sailors, especially those making long Pacific passages, carry devices for desalinating seawater as well. (We had, for emergency use, a Navy-surplus, solar water distiller.)

As to doctors and *medical emergencies*, good care is given in the larger towns in the hospital outpatient emergency room, inexpensively. Not only did I have the crushed finger X-rayed and sewed up expertly in France, but Bill had extensive dental work done in the American Hospital in Paris, as well as a tooth pulled by a kindly elderly dentist in Malta. However, the International Association for Medical Assistance to Travellers (IAMAT) was formed to "provide travellers with the names of centers in countries other than that to which they are native, and the names of locally licensed medical practitioners who have command of the native language spoken by the traveller and who agree to a stated and standard list of medical fees for their services." The association is worldwide, is supported by donations, and publishes a booklet listing member organizations and physicians. Its New York City address is: Empire State Building, 350 Fifth Avenue, Suite 5620, New York, N.Y. 10001. Medical assistance is available to ham radio operators by calling into international marine traffic nets like those found at 14.313 and 21.400 MHz. (If you sign a contract with a new company called Medical Advisory Systems, Inc., you can get some medical help by radio—for twenty dollars a minute.)

"Doctors" for *engines* and other *mechanical systems*, can usually be found in the larger towns. (Of course, foreign representatives for particular engines and equipment are often listed in the manuals or can be located through marinas or, sometimes, the telephone book.) But often by the time one reaches a big town, home remedies have had to be applied. An LDS sailor must become his own mechanic and innovator. Bill not only used his workshop equipped with AC converter to enable him to use power tools to reconstruct worn parts on the *Audacious*, but, in most ports, he was asked by someone to cut or drill some metal or to "lend" some engine part from his very redundant supply of replacements for everything that could go wrong—mechanical, plumbing, electrical, or rigging. In fact, it is common practice for LDS sailors to assist one another in making repairs.

There are always mysteries, though, where an *expert* is needed—particularly to fix the refrigeration or the electronics. Sometimes, asking around for help (even with the *Yachtsman's Eight Language Dictionary* compiled by Barbara Webb) may take several attempts or several unneeded repairs before, five hundred dollars later, the right thing is fixed. It can often save time to call the factory in the United States for a clue to what can be wrong. (Northstar simply sent out a new solid-state board to replace the faulty one in our LORAN, and we received it within a week.)

On the other hand, hidden geniuses can be found. On the way-out Bahamian island of Great Inagua, we followed local advice and called upon a Perkins Diesel tractor mechanic from the Morton Salt Company there, when our Westerbeke engine froze up (and this had meant a 190-mile crossing from the Dominican Republic in a sixty-knot gale without help from the engine). The tall, dignified black man (Mr. Ingraham) came down after work, took a look at the engine, and said, "Aha. Water in the cylinders." In one half hour he blew it out and freed the engine, though no one could figure out why it had happened, and it never occurred again. We met another genius at Man-O'-War Cay in the Abacos—Roy Russell—who saved us from having to buy a seven-hundred-dollar water pump by making a thirty-five-cent diversion in the line.

Keeping things working in the unfriendly environment of salt, water, and sun gives no rest to the captain (and no end to expense–living aboard is not cheap). It means checking, oiling, tightening up, and, unfortunately, replacing hoses, wires, fastenings, cotter pins, bushings, fuses, and so on, almost daily. Therefore, the boat is torn apart–seats out, tools all over, sawdust over everything–most of the time. Constant sanding, varnishing, and painting are required to keep the ship from turning gray beneath you, especially in the burning tropics.

Much time in port (or anchorage) is spent in this manner by LDS sailors rather than, say, in sightseeing. LDS sailors, on the other hand, see rather a different view of a town. They must *depend* upon the local townspeople and deal with them rather than merely observe them the way tourists do. In some ports–the Caribbean, Malta–locals come around each day, knock on the hull, and ask, "Hey, Skip. Hey, Skip. Any work? Good varnish and paint."

Then, in other ports–Mikonos, Yugoslavia, Martinique–there are some pleasant diversions from work, such as topless or nude crews aboard neighboring boats or on the beach.

Equipment bought in foreign ports–including paint, varnish, screws, and bolts–are often not true to size or color of their counterparts (even though the same number) in the States. Painting topsides, it is wise to use new paint for the whole job. (Equipment sent from the United States is subject to duty, unless used immediately on the boat.) Most LDS sailors find what they are looking for, however, whether it is sailmaker, compass adjuster, or just someone to climb the mast.

We have already talked about *charts*. One never goes wrong by stocking up for the next long segment of a trip where British Admiralty charts can be bought. When struggling to decide what ports to include (or what to use for alternatives if the weather should make it impossible to reach the ports of choice), it is always helpful to discuss a projected itinerary with others who have been there (after consulting guides like H. M. Denham's, for the Mediterranean countries and seas, or Kline's and Hart & Stone's for the Caribbean).

Weather broadcasts. Unfortunately, guides and government publications cannot always keep up with changes in frequencies and times of these most important broadcasts worldwide. A current copy of *Reed's Nautical Almanac* and the U.S. publication *Worldwide Marine Weather Broadcasts* will provide a good start on the problem. As the best weather broadcasts–like the Offshore and High Seas reports by the U.S. Coast Guard on North American weather, from Portsmouth, Virginia–are broadcast on SSB (single sideband) radio, a radio with this capability is helpful. However, provided you can discover where they are, there are excellent weather broadcasts given on regular AM frequencies in foreign countries (at least in Europe). Although they may be given in the language of the country, with only occasionally an English version, they are given in a simple form that can be easily followed by reference to the *Yachtsman's Eight Language Dictionary.* One difficulty, recently, has been, however, that strong Russian (and Cuban) stations near the weather stations overpower them. Certainly, a weather facsimile machine is a worthwhile luxury.

In French ports, and some Italian ones, weather information is posted in the harbor master's office. At any rate, as *harbor masters* and *immigration* and *customs* officers must be seen at each port, weather information can usually be found there. In Spain, however, the harbor master simply advised checking the daily newspaper for a weather map. In most countries, a cruising permit is provided at the first port of call, after payment of fees. In Turkey, the entry and departure formalities took a whole day for each one, but that is unusual. The permit will be relinquished on departure. Most harbor officials (all are smartly uniformed) are helpful and friendly, but on the Greek island of Kos, we were required to pay a fine for anchoring in the harbor, despite the fact that all berths along the quay were taken and a storm raged outside.

Knowing the *language* of a country, of course, makes all the difference (in Brindisi, Italy, the official advised trying to speak more Italian, "because it is a beautiful language"). But it is the difference between uttering isolated needs–"bread," "customs," "diesel,"–and discussing with other human beings the state of the world, the look of the weather. Most LDS sailors, therefore, try to form some phrases (using phrase books) and copy the correct accent so that the natives can understand. The attempt to use the language is appreciated and can start an interesting conversation, or find mutual friends and interests (unless the "foreigner" is more interested in trying out his English on you).

Finally, what about protection–that is, *firearms*? This is a subject for extensive LDS discussion, particularly in the last few years.

"I have a gun aboard, and I will protect my boat and my family," the owner of a Westsail-42 said.

"But could you really actually shoot someone?"

"If someone got aboard..." he began, and then told about the Pan American pilot and his wife anchored north of Andros in the Bahamas. They saw feet going by the cabin windows. The pilot went topside to find three natives on board, their dinghy tied astern. At first, the visitors appeared friendly, but then the oldest one put a knife to the pilot's throat and demanded money. His quick-thinking wife handed him a pistol. In the struggle for the gun, the pilot shot the man—dead. When the other two closed in, he shot them too. He immediately set off with the gruesome cargo for Nassau to report to government officials. (He was not held.)

"It was either him or them. That was quick thinking."

"But what about the thieves that come aboard at night in the French canals? They may steal all your lines and fenders but leave *you* alone," another skipper said.

A French girl pointed out, "Having a gun aboard can be a deterrent. Sometimes you only need to show it."

"Well," said a sailor from the Caribbean, "people at Pipe Cay used their gun—their flare gun—but they were killed."

"But you can't blab about seeing something funny going on over the radio," another Caribbean skipper pointed out.

"Lots of boats disappear, though, in all parts of the world—especially around Indonesia," the Westsail man continued. "It's best to be prepared. Have a gun and know how to use it—wisely."

And if you have one, it must be declared to customs.

All this comes under the heading of "running a tight little ship." It is part of the LDS sailor's satisfaction with his life mode to keep his boat clean and tidy and with all systems working. He wants a self-sufficient craft that is ready and able to engage in long passages, passages where he may meet menacing weather or pirates at sea or, perhaps, even a sunny, warm, and welcoming landfall where old friends will be found already at anchor in the quiet harbor.

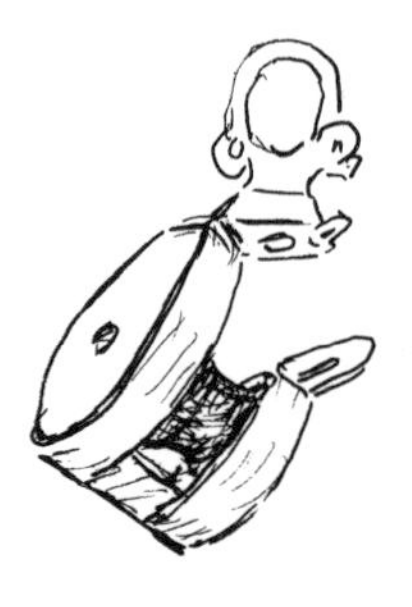

Snatch Block

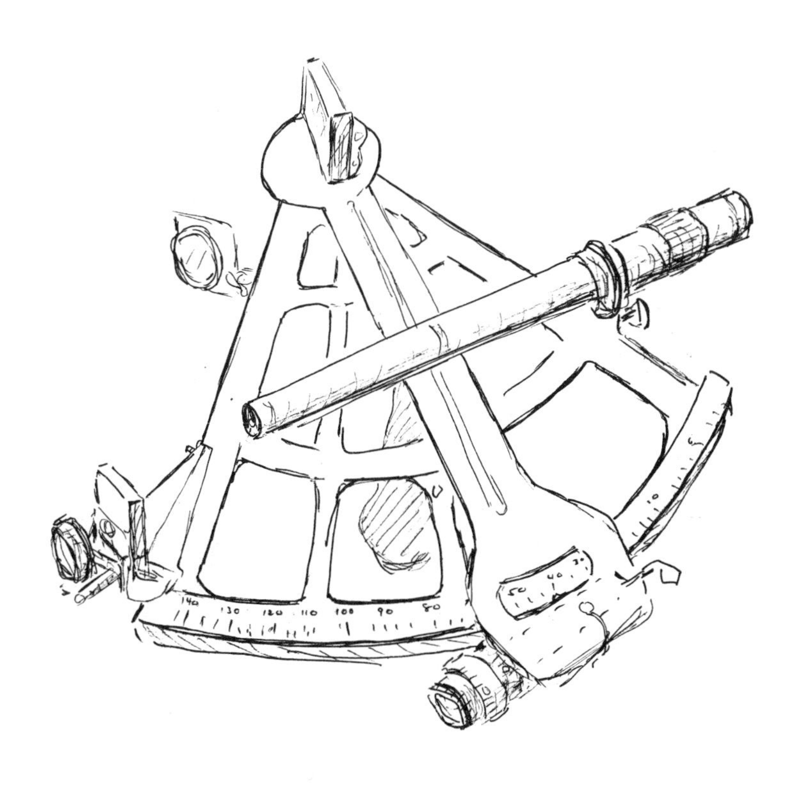

IX

Denizens of the Eastern Med

Sailing into the eastern Mediterranean means not only sailing into a new, strange opalescent light and mysterious dark seas, but sailing into antiquity, into the ghosts of long-ago myths and derring-do, into the beginnings of both Western and Eastern cultures. Everywhere are ancient man's monuments to gods, as well as to wars and trade.

The sun is hotter, the winds more violent, and even the sea itself is saltier (the Aswan Dam has appreciably cut back on the fresh water entering the Mediterranean here). Yet, there is the illusion of a languorous, easy life. Or so the bright advertisements—those featuring a lovely seminude leaning against a Doric column rising from the sea—would indicate. As Henry Miller wrote: "In Greece one has the desire to bathe in the sky. You want to rid yourself of your clothes, take a running leap and vault into the blue... or lie in the grass rigid and enjoy the cataleptic trance."

In May and early June it can sometimes be like that. At most other times, though, the winds from the north—the meltemi or boro boro—blow mercilessly down the mountains, across the seas, swirling around the islands, and there is no lee from them until a walled harbor is reached.

Captain H. M. Denham, in his *Sea-Guide to the Aegean and its Coasts and Islands*, warns, for instance, that "the vagaries of the winds prevent the Aegean being classed as an ideal sailing ground."

But he goes on to say that "the appeal of the small sheltered ports and anchorages together with scenery of bold and striking contrasts more than compensate." At any rate, sailors seem drawn to visit here. They usually explore Greek waters in the spring and early summer, the Turkish ports in the fall, and then winter in Cyprus or selected North African ports. (Popular Israeli or Lebanese or Libyan ports are, of course, out of the question now.) We found fewer American boats in these eastern waters than we found farther west. In fact, except for the ubiquitous charterer or the summer sailor, it is only the more dedicated LDS sailor who sails this far east in the Med.

Sailboart chartering is a fine-tuned business in Greece. In fact, only Greek flag boats can charter here. Charter fleets under other countries' flags must be based outside Greece in, say, Cypriot or Italian ports. Our first encounter with a Greek charter fleet was in Paxos, just south of the Ionian island of Corfu.

We had been asked to move away from the quayside which—as is characteristic of Greek island ports—was right along the Port Gayo village square and beside the church and an outdoor taverna. As an interisland cruise ship was due to tie up there, we dropped back among a fleet of twenty-four-foot sloops. There were thirteen of them. Two young men were readying them for the summer season, when they would be fully provisioned for two weeks and would travel in a group. The boys would be in a lead boat and the others would follow, learning navigation, sailing, and anchoring along the way. Those who passed muster would be allowed, on the twelfth day, to "solo"—sail to any of the Ionian islands they chose to, alone, and then return to Paxos by the final day. Later, we met some of the charterers on their solo sail to Levkas and found this appealed to them greatly. They liked sailing in company, and they felt more confident in sailing these strange waters after a week or so of group instruction. The charter company, on the other hand, could better protect their boats this way. When you consider the fact that even the Greek fishermen stay pretty close to shore along the Ionian Sea, you can see that this is a wise way to operate a charter business here.

There are similarly run fleets in the Aegean, most of them operating from Zea Marina in Piraeus, where 320 yachts are moored.

Of course, there are plenty of single boat charters as well, both bare-boat and with captain and crew.

We watched one charter company of ambitious and attractive young sailors in Zea Marina take a fleet of returning boats and, in just twenty-four hours, clean them, refuel them, fill their water tanks, completely provision them, and supply all necessary charts and guides for a new group of charterers to take away in the morning. This is a way of life for many young sailors (and older ones), from various countries. It is hard work, with lots of responsibility.

"Yes, we work hard, and we learn a lot about people," one of the girls told us. "But we're right on the scene, and sometimes can find good berths on some of the large charter boats for ourselves."

We were docked next to one of these large charter boats in Zea Marina. Named *Lely,* she was an old but beautifully kept dark blue schooner. Two Greek brothers worked on her constantly. We were to travel in her company when a family from Boston chartered her with her crew for a cruise among the Aegean islands.

In contrast, we later were moored beside a different type of charter boat—a large Turkish Mediterranean boat with high, wide bow, tall cabin, low masts for steadying sails, called *Princess Margaretta.* There was a large crew aboard her all day, but they habitually gathered about a table on deck under an awning and engaged in a loud game of cards. Toward evening, when it was cooler, they suddenly began to work—scraping and varnishing, tuning up the engine, rearranging the stores. At seven sharp in the evening, the owner would appear to examine the work's progress.

Finally, the first charter day arrived. A large assortment of passengers arrived, including two large dogs, plus bags and boxes and bicycles and kites and mattresses (apparently some were to sleep on deck). It took a while to get all this stored.

It was getting dark when the engine suddenly growled into action and ropes were cast off, amid loud instructions to all hands from the captain (the owner looked on with a worried look), and much running up and down the decks. With only a few rubs along the piles, they left, flags flying, smoke pouring aft from the funnel, and loud orders still being given. Two days later, they returned, still intact, but with everything at a much lower decibel level. The captain backed her in quietly, rushed the visitors and their gear off, and, when they were gone, collapsed in his chair beneath the awning. Unfortunately, we could not quite get his comments in Greek, but it was pretty evident that he was not looking forward to the next charter with much enthusiasm.

Zea Marina is the heart and crossroads of sailing in the eastern Mediterranean. Every sort you will ever see passes through here, and most every boat you have ever met.

Piraeus is the busy port of Athens. Its large northern commercial harbor berths freighters and tankers from every country of the world (many must anchor in the roadstead, to await their berth), and it accommodates all the ferries to outlying islands as well. There is no room for yachts here.

Zea Yacht Marina's inner harbor was originally Passalimini, a harbor planned in 493 B.C. by Themistocles for the protection of Athens from the Persians, and it, characteristically, reaches right into the city. In 1960, high stone breakwaters were built to extend the harbor. In this outer harbor, called Freatida, the large, gleaming white hundred-foot yachts—of Greek, Panamanian, and Liberian registry mostly—are berthed. Anything smaller is assigned to the inner harbor, where it is more protected and handier to all the facilities that encircle it. These include fancy restaurants whose delicious dishes are not only exhibited in the windows, but hawked by the restaurant personnel standing in the doorways.

A yacht captain must report to the marina office inside Zea to be assigned a berth. He must pay in advance, according to his tonnage, for a minimum of three days. Customs and immigration are taken care of by an agent from the main harbor. Usually, if he has just a moderate-sized boat, he will be told at first that there is no room. He then tries Tourkolimano where the Royal Hellenic Yacht Club is ensconced in a large and imposing white building, but he is not a member and therefore not welcomed there either. He tries across Phaleron Bay at Glifadha, near the Athens airport, but it is very unprotected there. And Vouliagmeni, ten miles below Piraeus, is almost always full. So he returns to Zea, quietly tying to another disappointed yacht, right at the entrance, to await a berth. However, from this vantage point, he is likely to see unexpected friends arrive or depart.

In fact, as we waited, we were delighted to see *Mimas* motor round the breakwater with sails furled, and, behind her, *Morning Haze*, the Belgian boat. They had come in from Malta, and it had been several months since we had seen them. We would have to catch up and trade tips on harbors to visit and those to avoid. We found that another old friend, *Phayet*, a forty-six-foot Tartan from South Africa and last seen in Crete, had arrived earlier and was already berthed in the inner harbor.

It happened that we had been aboard *Audacious* one year that very day, June 15. Anniversaries like that are always celebrated by LDS sailors. To celebrate, Doc and Nancy Gillies of *Mimas*, Leo and Gigi Colfs of *Morning Haze*, and Barbara and Pierre du Toit from *Phayet* came aboard. For such a gathering, ladies change from "sailing clothes" to more feminine attire, usually some native costume just purchased in the islands.

Although we were nearly touching neighbor boats on each side of us, we nevertheless achieved privacy in speaking different languages. To starboard were the Greeks aboard *Princess Margaretta*. To port were Germans. We were speaking English, with a few forays into French to converse with Gigi.

A charming Greek (and Italian) custom is to visit the quay in the evening. The whole town comes. It is an event. The girls dress up. The boys sometimes drive them in loud, fast cars, but usually all walk along briskly, talking loudly, sometimes asking questions of the people aboard boats. Often a group stops to fish. One evening, a young boy fishing next to us was doing a superb job of pulling in the fish. Several other boys stopped by, tossed in their lines, even borrowed some of the boy's bait, hoping to catch a fish there too, but with no luck. Still, the first boy merely dropped his hook, pulled a little, and there was another fish. All the while he chatted in a friendly manner to the others. He left with a full bucket, but no one else caught anything at all. A mystery.

While the Gillies' children joined the promenade aboard their folding motorbike, a typical LDS conversation followed in our open-air cockpit "patio."

"We had a tiresome trip, motored most of the way," from *Mimas*.

"You were lucky. A month earlier, we had rain and wind on the nose thirty days straight on the way here," from *Audacious*. "We came through the Corinth Canal, stopping at Delphi. Delphi was beautiful and fascinating, of course. I'm always amazed that those high pathways never have railings, the way they would in the United States. There were about twenty-five abandoned tankers anchored off Galaxidhi. Obsolete, they said."

"We came by Peloponnese, Spetsai and Aegina islands. Aegina has a nice harbor, but crowded, especially when the ferry is in, and you have to pay for water brought by cart."

"How much did you have to pay to go through the canal?"

"One thousand one hundred eighty-eight drachmas [1978]–and Denham said it would be a hundred three."

"Well, we came more or less nonstop for four hundred miles," Leo said, "and we were pretty tired. We've pretty well decided to buy a larger boat."

"Will you buy it here?"

"We'll go to an agent, I think, and keep in touch. I don't want to leave the boat here—even paying an agent to watch it, it would be risky."

"That's such a good sailing boat."

Leo translated for Gigi, and Gigi's answer was, "But it's wet and very cramped."

"I've got a problem with the dock master," Doc said. "Somehow the wrong documentation number got on the transit log I got at Zante [in the Ionian Sea], so I have to get that straightened out. I have to get a telegram from the Zante officials that I was there on that date. And my autopilot isn't working right, so I have to get that fixed. Then we'll go south to Crete."

"Where have you been since we saw you in Crete?" we asked Pierre and Barbara. They had owned a large plantation near Capetown, but things had not been going well. They decided to leave for a while. The only way they could take enough money out to live on was to represent South Africa in the Capetown to Rio Race, which they did. Once out, they had taken a tour of the United States East Coast, Britain, and the Mediterranean.

"We came up slowly through the Aegean," Pierre said. "While you went east and north, we went west and north. The boys are getting ready to take their exams at the Embassy here in Athens—exams like your college boards, I think. After that—and we hope they pass the first time—we'll probably go back to Crete for the winter. It's an interesting place. We like it. Then we'll think about what to do next."

"What about that young couple on that old Dutch boat, *Gastren*, that was between us in Iraklion?"

"Well, they decided to stay there. He was having trouble with the engine and needed some money to pay someone to fix it. So they are working as guides at Knossos, I think. They are always working on that old boat."

"It was fixed up like some kind of pirate's den below. Wonder if they'll ever get married. He wanted to take my ham radio apart and make it work better, but his radios didn't seem to be doing too well, so I held him off on that."

Then Nancy Gillies said, "The Manns [*Flapper II*] and the Motts [*Deniz Agaci*] should be coming down the Gulf of Corinth as you are going up on your way to Yugoslavia. They were going there before coming to Greece."

"They'll be here, then, while the meltemi is very strong. What about the Haydens?"

"They're staying in Malta. They might move out to Cyprus for the winter. Al is doing a few portraits, and selling them. And Lou is selling her jewelry. Al had a lot of work to do on the boat before leaving, he says. Maybe they'll stay in Malta for another winter."

They showed us the beautiful and sensitive drawings Al had done of their children. We hoped he was asking for his portraits what they were really worth.

We talked on until twilight faded into darkness and the promenade had thinned to only a few walking couples. As our friends left, we wondered, after our short visit here, when we would see them again and whether, in fact, we would ever all be together again. Yet, it is not so different from everyday life on land, is it? All our human contacts are tenuous and temporary.

It was around midnight that night that we had another visitor. We heard a loud knock on the transom and struggled up to see what was the matter.

"Do you need a crew?" came a young girl's voice.

No, we did not. This had been happening all day, as it does to all boats that look well taken care of. It happened on Malta as well.

"I just need a lift to Italy," or Spain, or whatever.

We talked to a couple who said yes to one of these hitchhikers.

"Once aboard, he was seasick right away and could not help at all—probably from drugs. But he demanded all kinds of special foods and accused us of feeding him the wrong things and of sailing the boat badly. Later, he tried to sail the boat to Bari, when we were headed for Brindisi. He helped himself to liquor and food, and at night I was afraid to go to sleep. It was harrowing. When, at last, we arrived in Brindisi, we found we were short about one hundred dollars in cash. But we have heard that some people have been killed and their boats stolen by these boat hitchhikers."

We stayed on in Zea for a while to catch up on our boat maintenance. The cruel sun and thick salt grind at the varnish so that it seems to crack and peel as you watch it. But it was so hot in June there (over one hundred degrees) that we would do our sanding right at daybreak, then put on the varnish late in the afternoon.

Before we left, we saw another familiar boat enter the harbor—*Far Horizons*—and we heard from her news of what it was like to sail in Egypt, Israel, and Lebanon. Not that everyone would approach these countries exactly the way the MacGregors would.

"We were headed for Alexandria from Malta," Jim said, "but we ended up in Crete, finally. We went over to Alexandria later. What a disappointment. The harbor was filthy. Everything was expensive, and the officials wouldn't let us alone. But I wanted to take the kids to see the Pyramids. The harbor in Tel Aviv is beautiful, really beautiful, but we were told to leave. A gunboat ushered us out and followed us along the coast of Lebanon until we were beyond that country. Several other boats followed us, too, and one fired across the stern to warn us."

"The children were scared. They go below now every time a powerboat comes close."

"Why did you try to go to Lebanon?"

"I didn't think we'd be back here soon, so I wanted to see Israel and the Holy Land and the rest. I didn't think they'd bother a sailboat. Also, we needed food. We'd bought a lot of canned tuna – got a good price and took a hundred dollars' worth – so we had that, but nothing fresh. We went on to Cyprus then, and that was really nice, but it took quite a long time. And we kept looking back for our escort."

Far Horizons was heading westward, heading for Gibraltar and then the Caribbean.

"We'll probably see you along the way somewhere," but we did not see them again until we arrived in St. Thomas, V.I., and that was to be the last time.

A small, neat powerboat backed into the quay beside us. It belonged to a cousin of the captain of the *Princess Margaretta*. The captain of the *Princess* had never run a charter boat before, he told us, and he was not sure it was going to work out. He and his wife invited us out to a "real Greek dinner." He was Captain Constantinos (Gus) Tassis of Coast Shipping Enterprises, and they lived in Athens. He was dark, soft spoken, of military bearing; she was blond, talkative, warm. But it was Gus who felt at home with English. I struggled in rudimentary Greek with his wife, Dia.

Dressed in our party clothes – always a bit wrinkled coming from the cramped boat locker – we accompanied them to the balcony of a distinguished restaurant overlooking the Tourkolimano yacht harbor. Beyond the twinkling lights in the harbor were the lights of Athens' suburbs. Below us was the colorful evening promenade.

Our first stop was the kitchen. It is a courtesy in Greece to examine the food before ordering it—and to exclaim on its beauty and the cleanliness of the kitchen. We chose hors d'oeuvres and Greek salad to begin, a course of broiled shrimp (in their jackets), a course of fresh-caught snapper, and dessert of fresh fruit (watermelon, cherries, and apricots) and coffee and liqueur.

Though our view was of fairyland, Gus spoke seriously and revealingly to us. Greece was just beginning to recover from the rule of the generals and her Cypriot problems, he said, but the United States—through the CIA—was doing continual mischief in the Mediterranean countries. Perhaps we did not know. It was the CIA, he said, who backed the Red Brigades in Italy in order that the army (Italian) could take over. And it was the CIA who stirred up the trouble in Cyprus, of course. Although they were both most charming, we were now certainly aware that, except for our tourist dollars, we were not really friends of Greece. Rather, we (meaning Americans in general) are innocents abroad, blithely enjoying the fruits of the centuries of culture and the beauties of the scenery, while having little understanding of the real political turmoil going on beneath the surface here.

Gus pointed out, also, the lack of crime in Greece (and even in Yugoslavia) because, he said, the family and the Catholic religion were still strong. He noted, as well, the contrast between the visiting yachtsmen and the island poor, who subsisted upon the fish and goats and olives that they raised on the arid soil.

As to drugs—there was no leniency here. Yes, we told Gus, we had seen commandeered boats, from small sailboats to large, rusty freighters with windows shot out, tied in harbors to rot, their owners (of any nationality) languishing in jail. And we noticed, too, the number of naval ships—of all nations—on maneuvers in the Med (even in 1978–9).

But, like most Long Distance Sailing sailors, we were observers, people almost without a country, moving ever on, looking, tangling with the elements, learning a little about how people live along the Mediterranean Sea.

Other than the charter groups, most sailors in the eastern Med travel alone, planning their day's runs so that a practical itinerary of sightseeing is achieved while keeping to routes with some protection from prevailing winds and that end in safe and pleasant harbors for the night. That is the plan. The fact that it does not seem to work out that way in these waters explains the care taken by sailors here.

For example, we left tall Kea Island (the island with the stone lion) in the Aegean early one morning, in the company of *Lely* and others, to cross to Siros, the capital of the Cyclades. But as we rounded Kea's northern tip, dark clouds gathered in, bringing strengthening south winds and rain (not according to the weather forecast for that day). Soon, the Mediterranean was riled into its characteristic sharp accordion-pleated seas. We shortened sail and used our engine, but could make no headway southward–even in the lee of Yioura (the prohibited prison island). In fact, the wind whistled down its mountainsides in williwaws. We had to change our destination to Tinos, where we were able to sail on a broad reach. We slid through the narrow opening between Andros and Tinos into the somewhat protected harbor of Panormos–a small village which exports its quarried green marble. Two small French boats were already tied to the quay with many lines, and their owners helped us secure *Audacious*. We exchanged experiences for a while, then each of us settled down in his own craft for the night.

Suddenly a knock sounded on the hull. We looked out the hatch to see a man from the village.

"I see you are from New York," he said. "I just came from the States. I worked at Sperry on Long Island for a while. Now, I'm back here with a little money, to live in my home village of Panormos."

Bill knew a few of the people at Sperry that he knew.

"What are you doing now that you're back in Greece?" Bill asked him.

"Oh," he said, "I'm retired. I live on the Social Security checks from the States." And he added, "Lots of Greeks go to the States to earn money for their old age." (Good old U.S.A.)

Another bout with the violent winds in Greece ended in a different kind of experience–one that prepared us for the ubiquitous nudes to be seen on the beaches in Yugoslavia, our next country.

We had left Corinth (after a bus trip to see Schliemann's excavations at Mycenae) in a moderate northwest wind. This meant we had to tack back and forth to make any headway up the Gulf of Corinth toward Galaxidhi and Delphi. The wind strengthened, however, and the seas sharpened up. The boat began to pound, heel, and take solid water across the decks.

On our first tack, we expected to make the entrance to a small bay where there would be a lighthouse (lighthouses in Greece are small, white matchsticks on rocky promontories, which show up fairly well, if they are not in the shadow–though not as well as the many little white churches dotted over even the wildest and barest of terrains). We did not make the landfall, however, and there was only a featureless, solid mountain wall stretching as far as we could see in both directions. We tacked out into the gulf again, hoping for something on shore to show up when we tacked back in, to give us a clue to how far down the gulf we had come.

Meanwhile, the boat was laboring, it was getting late, and we were tired. I studied the charts, searching for some kind of landmark, height of terrain, indentations, or towns, but there was only the five-thousand-foot, reddish mountain rampart. Measuring again our estimated track, I thought we might be close to a fjord into Aspra Spitia, a bauxite processing port. Denham's guide said its lighthouse was difficult to see in the daytime, but that there was a series of two lights (on Cape Mounda and Tsaruchi Point). We watched (and hoped) for them. At last, a faint flash, then another showed against the rock, and we sailed into a dark, windless, deep anchorage, finally anchoring for the night at midnight.

In the morning, we started off again for Galaxidhi. But once again, the gulf wind was just as strong, as we nosed into a landlocked little bay on the point below Galaxidhi called Andromaki, and dropped anchor. That evening, out of the stillness of the surrounding arid but aromatic hills, came the sound of many low bells. We came up on deck to see a picture from the past. Coming over the hill was a flock of nearly a hundred goats and sheep. The goats were large, dark brown, and belled in the deeper tones; the sheep had the soprano bells. With them strode two shepherds, with their wooden crooks and long woolen ponchos. Sheep dogs hurried the flock along and kept stragglers on the path. We watched them cross the beach and climb the hill on the other side to what apparently was the night pasture. A donkey on the hillside called to them. In the early morning, the flock returned, the goats with the deep bells leading, the rest following on.

As the wind continued to blow, we remained at Andromaki. Another small boat came in, but anchored farther in, behind a little rise.

We started working on the boat—there are always chores—but later noticed two people on the beach. They were idly wading, it was warm and quiet there, and they were nude. Naturally, we watched them curiously. After a short dip, they walked back up the beach and lay down together. The girl languorously lifted her leg across the boy, and, as we watched, they became more entwined and animated in the complete act of love. Finally, they lay back for a cozy nap. But just a short one, for they went in for another dip and wash-off and returned to the beach for another bit of lovemaking.

All in all, it had been a most *pastoral* Greek anchorage.

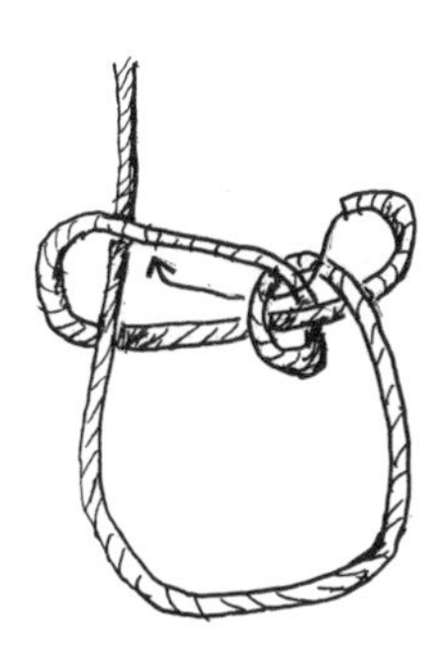

Some bouts with excessive winds, though, are not the usual solo horror-encounters, but can throw boats together in a humorous way. At one island in particular – Santorini (or Thira) – it is possible to find boats from eight different countries banging together for a whole night.

Santorini is a group of islands that forms the shell, or caldera, of a great volcano that exploded around 1500 B.C. The great eruption dropped tons of rosy ash on Thira and on Crete, over sixty miles away, so much, in fact, that their legendary Minoan culture was buried and lost. (Some say that Santorini was the mythical Atlantis, but others point out that Plato's reference to Atlantis places it ten thousand years earlier.)

One sails now inside the outside crater walls. They are high, dark, and bare of vegetation, with white villages atop them that appear as snow from offshore. Several hundred feet below Thira village, in an indentation in the steep wall, is a stone quay. Leading up from it is a zigzag donkey track to the village. There is room for eight yachts, all of whom must fasten stern lines to a single large red mooring buoy, and bow lines to the quay. After completing this maneuver, we watched while several yachts fought for the last space, at the same moment that caïques from five large cruise ships anchored offshore were shuttling passengers in to take the donkey ride up to the tourist shops in the village above.

That night, a strong south wind raised sharp seas that broke against the quay and the stern of each boat. The wind took sail covers and even one rubber dinghy right up and over the line of boats. No manner of retying or fendering could keep the boats from smashing against one another all night. And boat skippers tramped about their decks, each cursing in his own language.

Next morning, the French boat next to us pulled out (taking our docking lines with him). We backed out (just as a single-hander tried to come in), performing like a spider disentangling herself from a web of rope. That night we spent in the black moonscape of the still-smoking crater island itself—the small island called Nea Caemene, in the very center of the caldera. As it was too deep for us to anchor, we tied to a German boat which was tied to a small dock. They came aboard for drinks, and we talked about the early days of the movies in a mixture of English, German, French, and Italian.

Sailors to the eastern Mediterranean have a choice. Either they remain here for years, caught in the spell of the elusive antiquity or the mysterious light and silence, or, simply, the easy, inexpensive living. Or, like us, they must start westward in order to reach Gibraltar for a November crossing to the Caribbean. Some disappear down the Red Sea to sail eastward.

There is always so much more that should be seen besides the well-known, well-documented architectural and artistic treasures. There are places like Bodrum, Turkey, where, despite the endless game of customs forms, there is a virility and foreignness in its scenes of pantalooned women washing their sheep in the harbor waters, of camels as the form of transportation to the lively marketplace manned by brigands with long black mustaches. Or tiny forgotten islands like Denoussa, visited by few yachts, where the wind blows hard into every harbor, where there is a village with no roads, no electricity, no telephone, but a large white church, and where the hills are covered with the prickly, aromatic maquis bushes that tell of the presence of a Greek island almost before it can be seen and the valleys are shaded by the silver-gray olive trees.

One can only hope it will be possible to return.

Mediterranean Windmills

X

Night Sailors

It is easy to become rapturous about night sailing, though most of it is rough, cold, and downright frightening. Yet it is a fact of life in Long Distance Sailing, where distances ahead are long and must be reckoned with. For, in order to make a difficult landfall in the daylight, most long passages must be made through the night.

Europeans make crossings like the English Channel at night, preferring to navigate from major light to major light, even if it means lying off the landfall until dawn. The fact that most ships and tankers traverse the Channel at night does not seem to bother them. Cruise ships plying between, say, Brindisi and Corfu, or between Caribbean islands, move at night also, while their passengers are asleep, and, as they are often wasting time, their courses are slow and rather wandering – or so it seems to a passage-making sailboat trying to keep out of their way.

Fishing boats of every country, though usually brightly lighted for work on deck, are apt to cross back and forth across a sailboat's course in their business of trawling for fish, with little notice given to other craft with other business in the area. And if there is a fleet of them out there, sorting out the directions and distances and intentions of these lighted boats can be harrowing, particularly when nets are stretched behind them, as well as to poles with dull, or even no lights. Nowadays, there is the new danger of unlighted but fast-moving boats who are also habitual night travelers, transporting contraband of one kind or another. And among all these, the sailboat skipper must be alert for the boat with three vertical white lights that identify it as a tug with a tow.

Mix all these in a brew of fog or heavy squall and you have a true sailor's nightmare. Especially so when you realize that sailboats are run down by ships at sea more often than reported statistics show.

Of course there are aids to night navigation.

A sailing boat skipper can hang one of several types of radar reflectors in his rigging. These are actually radar reflector "enhancers"—they make the pip of your boat on another boat's radar screen bigger and more noticeable than it would normally be. Another type is called a radar "detector"—many single-handers have these. It lights up a warning indicator to show a solid something—boat or shore—at a particular distance and bearing from your boat.

Radar on your boat will show the small pips that are moving boats on your screen—provided it is working and showing the proper range. Our discussions with other LDS skippers about radar have brought to light these thoughts: radar is fine in confined harbors (short range), provided it has been operating constantly and is therefore working; otherwise a radar technician is needed to keep it dependable. It is unwise to depend on other ships' seeing you on *their* radar screens, because their radarman may either not be watching or simply be unable to pick you up, as you are below his level of scan. (Of course, these are worst-case conditions only.)

These conditions are similar to those that limit dependence upon an automatic pilot. Unless you have been operating it regularly and are confident it is dependable, it may well wander off on its own course while the skipper sleeps. We had one, for instance, that worked wonders—for about twenty minutes. But even if it had worked well, Bill would always want someone's eyes watching 360 degrees in the cockpit at all times. Of course single-handers do not have the luxury of that choice and must depend on either mechanical self-sailers like the Ariel or electronic autopilots like Tillermaster—plus a warning horn on their radar detector indicators.

Beyond the standard light equipment aboard—navigation lights, masthead light, spreader lights, compass light, navigation-table light, and a working flashlight, one more light on deck is usually in the LDS sailor's equipment—a searchlight, for shining on the sail when approaching other vessels; on other vessels themselves, on buoys, shorelines, and, in case of unwelcome boarders, in their eyes.

Even equipped with these aids, however—plus an operating LORAN, RDF, or satellite navigator—nighttime at sea adds another dimension. On watch at night, you long for first light. And on the first watch, you hang on to the twilight, reassuring yourself that it is not yet dark, when, in truth, it already is. You promise yourself that when the friend over your shoulder, the lighted moon, sets, the starshine will be there to ease the enclosing night darkness. You even grasp at the phosphorescence in the waves tossed off by the hull. Surely it will add the reassurance of light.

But as the watch stretches to hours, the night sea hypnotizes you. Alone in the cockpit, your hands on the wheel, your eyes shift from the red compass light—the ship's heart—to the masthead in the stars, to the bow slicing into the night. The red and green navigation lights flicker in the spume, and the waves roar off the stern. For hours, the boat grinds on, like a horse galloping through the night over wild terrain. There's the swish and splash of waves, the fire of the phosphorescence where they break. Slowly, the boat begins to feel as though it is above the water, as though it has broken the bond that keeps it on the sea. As it rolls with the waves, it is a bird balancing, dancing in its course forward. It seems to have a mission that presses it forward, with full speed. The boat is a living thing communicating with the sea and the night.

A sudden slat is the first sign the wind has slacked off. Finally, trimming sheets does no good and all the sails are lowered except the mainsail. It is quieter, and your thoughts address what makes this vessel what it is. With no one around to censure you, you silently express your gratitude to this vessel pushing on through the night. You thank the man who designed her so skillfully, the men who built her so faithfully, those who carefully put together her engine, her sails, her instruments. You see in her the living wood of trees, the warmth of sunlight, and her response to the pull of the forces of the water, of the earth and of the moon.

Meanwhile, you are shivering from sitting out in the damp, cold darkness and from allowing yourself to listen to the voices of the night. For there are sighings that come across the water—perhaps whales talking. And there are flutterings from passing birds (some land on the deck). And splashes from porpoises swimming like guards beside the boat.

It is time to stand and take a 360-degree survey for lights that may be boats approaching. If there is one, it must be examined through the binoculars. Is there a green or a red light? A low and a high white light? Three vertical white lights? Its progress must be carefully monitored. Then, quickly, below, a LORAN reading and a D.R. (dead reckoning) measurement must be entered on the chart and in the log, using as little light as possible in order not to wake the sleeper(s).

Then, suddenly, you realize the wind has strengthened. The sail is full, and again you are tearing through the night. Waves begin to splash on the deck. Spray, then solid water, comes across the cockpit. Looking out across the water, the moonlight plays over the surface, painting it molten silver but hiding the true contour in its mercurial patterns. Looking toward the black shore, it is impossible to tell the distance, impossible to tell if, in fact, it is the shore that is there. The picture of stability and sureness is beginning to fall apart and a cold fear creeps in. You wish for your relief to come up. You wish for a cup of coffee. You wish for your warm bunk below.

Finally, the off-watch, hearing the new noise of the sail and feeling the increased motion, relieves you early. Sails are readjusted and the spell is broken. But even in your bunk, the wild exhilaration in the night fills your mind and keeps you from falling asleep right away. Yet you must sleep. In another few hours it will be your turn to take the helm again.

It is small wonder that night sailing sometimes becomes disorienting, particularly when just two, husband and wife, are sharing the duty.

We have been confused often enough, especially on nights when squalls and thick weather alternated with a brilliant moon popping in and out of clouds, completely changing the look of things.

Perhaps the best disorientation story involved *Venture*, a ketch owned and built by the Wood family from Lake Michigan. They had come all the way down the Mississippi (in fact, they were still, with a workbench on deck, putting last-minute touches on her cabin on the way), had crossed the Gulf and were on the way across the Atlantic. Very conscious of the fact that they had to steer well north of Cuba's territorial waters, they nevertheless misidentified a sea buoy at night, and were not as far off as they thought they were. Toward dawn, they spotted two high-speed boats approaching. Soon it was evident that they were gray Cuban gunboats, and heading for *them*.

"We wondered what they were up to . . . whether war had been declared while we'd been out there sailing," they told us.

The gunboats drew alongside the *Venture* and ordered her to stop. The Woods struggled with the sails, nervous about what was going to happen next. Several uniformed officers carrying carbines jumped aboard the boat and took over the controls. They would answer no questions. Under power, *Venture* followed the gunboats south toward Cuba. The Woods did not know whether they had been hijacked by pirates or were being commandeered by the Cuban Coast Guard.

In Havana, they were told they had been five miles within the limit of Cuban waters, their boat would be taken over, and they would probaby have to go to jail while the boat was cleared. That could be a very long time. Although the Woods, who knew no Spanish, tried to explain it was just a navigation error and that they were just a family in their own boat trying to sail the Atlantic, it made no difference. Nor were they allowed to contact the United States Embassy or Guantanamo Naval Base in Cuba. Sentries were assigned. The radios in the main cabin were removed. The Woods waited.

After a day or two, the Wood boys found that the Cuban sentries enjoyed rock music (they had been allowed to keep the stereo). Meanwhile, one of the boys discovered an old VHF radio in the aft cabin and was able to fix it. While the boys turned the rock and roll up loud, he was able to get a message to Guantanamo. After that, the way was cleared for them to leave.

Another boat involved in a night experience that is not uncommon, and one not involving storm conditions, was *Mimas*. Coming from the Canaries, her landfall at Antigua came at night. Her crew made out a strong light ahead, not quite on her course, but with associated lights that appeared to be lights from buildings on land. When lights appeared to the north, they took them for Barbuda, north of Antigua. Fortunately, the current was against them, rushing out between the islands, for at dawn it became evident that they were sailing straight into Montserrat and those lights to the north had been Antigua.

Even after a perfectly quiet, languorous, moonlit night when the boat plows a field of phosphorescence and the sails nod in the dome of stars overhead, the coming of the dawn always gives a feeling of reassurance and hope—as well as clarifying one's position.

XI
The Westward Trek

Before August 1, those planning a westward passage across the Atlantic for a winter in the warm Caribbean start leaving the eastern Med for Gibraltar.

The large charter boats will leave their lucrative European summer chartering waters for their more lucrative Caribbean charters. And those globe-trotting sailors who have completed their tour of the Mediterranean will slowly move to the west, to explore new seas and islands. Some, to be sure, will be tempted by Ischia, Majorca, or Spanish ports like Puerto Jose Banus to spend another winter in the Med. And some, as we shall see later, will never leave Gibraltar.

All these boats moving west will follow almost the same westward path: from Greece to Yugoslavia, to Italy and Sicily, across to Sardinia and the Balearics, and along Spain's south coast to Gibraltar. They choose the northern shore of the Med because the easterly currents are not as strong against them as they are along the African coast.

The first gathering point—indeed, the doorway from the elusive East to the busy, modern West—is Corfu, in the westernmost of Odysseus' "wine-dark seas," the Ionian. In contrast to the arid

Aegean islands, Corfu (or Kerkira) is luxuriantly wooded, lush with both wild and cultivated flowers, and undergoing development. It has always been a crossroad. Naval ships, including those destined for the Peloponnesian Wars in the fifth century B.C. and, later, those bound from Europe to defeat the Turks at Lepanto in the sixteenth century A.D., all passed through Corfu waters. In more recent times, Corfu has been under the sovereignty of Venice (whose influence is evident in its architecture, gardens, and harbor walls), of France, Britain, even Yugoslavia and Germany (briefly), before finally reverting to Greece. Now, it is the jumping-off place for Brindisi and western Europe.

What an assortment of vessels here: large luxury yachts (like the Onassis *Christina*), many with small cars or even helicopters on deck; large charter auxiliaries (like *Sea Star of Hebrides* and *Marie Pierre* from Malta); innumerable racing and cruising sailboats of every vintage, as well as Greek caïques and modern Italian cruise ships.

We were invited aboard one of the hundred-foot power yachts one day–one with a car–the *Jamie II*, of U.S. registry. We were shown carpeted "rooms" with lamps, paintings on the walls, and knickknacks on the tables. (Later, through the ports, we saw silk nightclothes laid out on turned-down beds.) The owner, a New York furniture manufacturer, was not aboard. The only passengers were a couple who had won a contest to sell the greatest amount of the owner's furniture in their own retail store. The boat was run by a captain (based in Grenada in the Caribbean) and a mixed crew of handsome blacks and tall blondes, both male and female, and we noticed that they worked hard all day. As the captain preferred sailboats, he said, he and the winning couple came "slumming" aboard our sailboat for a general discussion of other boats in the harbor and of Mediterranean ports on Spain's south coast. The boat with the helicopter, the captain told us, would not be crossing the Atlantic. Its owner disliked ocean passages, so he had another boat, similarly equipped, waiting for him in the Caribbean.

Moving ever westward, yachts planning to visit Yugoslavia from Greece must first go to Italy (usually Brindisi), then recross the unfriendly Adriatic, because Albania and Albanian waters are closed to visitors. In fact, pilot boats are always lying off its shores.

We were told the sad tale of one yachtsman who lost both his mast and his engine during a storm in the Corfu North Channel. After several days, thinking himself lucky, he coasted into the

Albanian port of Butrinto. But his boat was immediately taken into custody and he was detained. Although he got away himself, he was still in court, trying to get his boat out after several years of haggling.

(Another sad story was told about the North Channel. A fellow going north, making for Brindisi, was below while his daughter steered his new forty-eight-foot Hinkley. She called down to ask him which side of a buoy to go, but too late. No one had checked the chart. The boat hit the rocks and sank in forty feet of water on a quiet, sunny morning. Now there is another buoy, marking the wreck.)

Brindisi, on the Adriatic, is an ancient Italian city. Before Alexander the Great and the Roman Caesars, the Assyrian Queen Semiramis ruled over her "Empire of Ninus." The Appian Way started here, and Phineas Fogg departed from Brindisi for his eighty-day trip around the world. The city climbs a hill, its stone buildings intertwined with climbing steps, and opening unexpectedly on open squares. Tiny shops, more frequented by the natives but happily discovered by roaming sailors, are tucked in the ground floors of buildings, turning up by surprise with no advertisement of their presence. A butcher shop was behind a curtain of beads, and there was a bakery where two men in white caps were covered with flour.

This must be the world's noisiest city. The main square is always filled with tourists waiting for cruise ships to depart. And yachts from every country are moored along the quay, stern to. Twenty-four hours a day, cars, trucks, and motorcycles roar along the quay, horns blowing. Billions of swallows arc around the tops of buildings, in some endless, noisy game of tag. We saw *Sea Star of Hebrides* again, this time waiting for a final charter for summer. A German boat tried to crowd in beside us, unsuccessfully, but as he roared away from the quay he caught our anchor and would have pulled the stern out of our boat if strong, yelling onlookers had not kept our lines taut. At last he backed down.

We found another American retiree craft, the *Atcha*, a small green Fischer, which was going our way. The Sechels from Massachusetts had just retired from the Aeronautical School at Princeton. We asked Mrs. Sechel how she liked her new life.

"Living aboard the boat all the time is just too boring," she said. "I leave for a while and then come back."

A couple whose cruise ship had oversold and left them behind (he went to Vassar, she to Yale) came aboard to use our head, and to tell us how the cruise ships *always* oversold and also required, at the last minute, an unadvertised restamping of tickets. For those left behind, there was no place to sleep but in the square, on the stone.

"Boy, I'd be afraid to cross the ocean in *that* boat," they said.

Meanwhile, in Brindisi's outer harbor, two U.S. Naval helicopter carriers were running exercises involving low-level passes across the harbor.

Usually, sailors pressing westward plan to limit their stay in Yugoslavia, but, once there, are entranced by the green offshore islands with their villages of red-roofed houses nestled in bustling little harbors, and by the old walled cities on the mainland. Probably their most popular yachting stops are the fjordlike Gulf of Kotor (sailors have been hauled in and interrogated here for photographing the submarine pens being built back into the mountainsides), Dubrovnik, the old capital of Montenegro, and the walled city of Split—plus, of course, the long string of offshore islands (particularly Korcula, Marco Polo's birthplace, and the jolly port of Hvar). Not many have time to go all the way to Trieste.

An added attraction to the colorful offshore islands is the large number of nude bathers on their long white beaches. We noticed that wherever a German boat was anchored, a pair of binoculars could spot nudes on shore. Amusingly enough, the children wore bathing suits. The nudes lay about the beach and on rocks, like seals, or played strenuous games of ball or tag. Once back aboard their boat, small bikinis were donned by the ladies and garments dubbed by our daughter "parts sacks" by the men. All the bodies thus clothed, or unclothed, were not handsome. We would watch them parade along the quay outside our cabin ports, their thighs jiggling, tummies bulging, but all tanned to a crisp. Perfectly comfortable. But of course it was not always Germans—there were sun worshippers on boats from every country.

We were surprised that most of the beaches that stretch along Yugoslavia's shores and along her islands were crowded and bright with umbrellas during the summer. The face that Yugoslavia shows to boaters is not the austere, subdued one expected in an Eastern Bloc country.

Modern hotels graced most every prominent point, as well. These were built in tiers of windows (rather like typewriters) with outside glassed-in elevators and grand beach facilities. We were told that these were worker vacation hotels, to which workers were assigned on specified dates. The restaurants were open to the public. Privately owned restaurants – like other private businesses – could remain in private ownership until they had six or more employees. Then the state took over. Although there were many new stores and a bustling population, sailing people found market shelves held mostly pastas of different kinds and cans of entrails in tomato sauce. Fresh-food open-air markets, as in all Europe, offered more. And the meat markets did a lively business.

But, in spite of the visibly busy towns full of tourists – both native and foreign – individual Yugoslavs expressed real concern about the "after Tito" stability among the three rival provinces, Montenegro, Dalmatia, and Croatia. An uninvited visitor to the boat surreptitiously asked Bill to take a package out of the country. If he had, it could have brought real trouble for all of us.

Like most yachts, we stopped in Dubrovnik. The port officials were courteous and helpful. Though they took away the ship's papers and passports for examination, they returned them promptly. The best marina in Dubrovnik is Gruz Marina, where fuel, water, and laundry service were supplied. There we saw the Sechels and *Atcha* again, and met Mary and Bill Black from Seattle on *Foreign Affair,* their Valiant-40.

"I used to be in the lumber business," Bill told us, "and we decided to take two years and go around the world – if we could. We had to sell everything to get this expensive boat, but for this trip we wanted a good one."

We nodded. They were an attractive dark-haired couple, soft-spoken, humorous, probably a little younger than we.

"We did a lot of studying, though there's always something more you wish you'd done. As a matter of fact, the day we left we had a big going-away party with about fifty people aboard. But I still had things on my list to do. One was to check the bilge pumps, so I opened the sea cocks in preparation. But someone handed me a drink and I forgot about turning on the pumps until someone pointed out we were standing ankle deep in water. Luckily the bilge pumps *did* work."

They told us about their trip across the Pacific and then up the Red Sea and into the Mediterranean. Mary did not think of the Red Sea the way Roy and Rika of *Honnalee* had, though.

"I wouldn't have missed it for anything," she said. "There was this alien land and unfriendly people on both sides. I felt it was the most foreign place we'd been."

Their boat, like *Honnalee,* was also decorated with Eastern things–rugs, pillows, artifacts–and many books.

"You're going through the Panama Canal, then," we said.

"We hope not. We plan to go through the Strait of Magellan at Cape Horn. But we will only do it if our sons are able to join us at that time."

We smiled to ourselves then, but of course they did just that, and then circled up to Alaska as well, before returning to their home port of Seattle. We were surprised, as we had wrongly considered them rather new to sailing. We underestimated their curiosity, stamina, and perseverance. They were, in fact, to win the Cruising Club of America Blue Water Medal for that voyage.

The Gruz Marina people urged us all (our friends Janet and Larry Mead were aboard then) to go to a symphony concert to be held in the cathedral square in the old city of Dubrovnik. This part of the city is walled with ramparts built by the Venetians to keep out the Serbs and Croatians and Hungarians, as well as the Turks. Now, the old harbor is silted in, and all vehicles are excluded from inside the walls. The walkways are patterned stone and crowded with people. For the concert, bleachers had been set up all around the central square. They backed up against dwellings, so that shuttered windows opened on the rows of seats. We watched two old crones gazing out of their windows for a free concert, and high up across the orchestra, which was in the center, a large cat in a lighted window stretched and tiptoed tantalizingly at the very edge of the sill. A crowd of noisy swallows swung through the courtyard with loud complaints, too. The excellent concert, we noticed, was all music of Eastern composers.

Although boats from many nations sail the Dalmatian coast, we met only one old friend, even after searching each harbor carefully. At our last stop in Yugoslavia, Rogac Cove, in the national park on the western tip of Mljet Island, we found our British friends from Malta, the Brookes, on their boat *Papingo.* Rogac Bay, contrary to what our R.C.C. Folio had predicted, was full of boats. Ninety percent of them were headed west, but the Brookes were heading east, to Cyprus, rather than to Gibraltar.

"We've rather made our commitment," they said. "We've everything we own now, either aboard *Papingo* or in our flat in Malta.

But we may make a trip back to England someday. Who knows."

Aboard for a drink, we heard that the Haydens were still in Malta working on *Honeybird* when the Brookes left late in the summer; that the Bartons were in Greece on *Rose Rambler,* and that *Marie Pierre* would be crossing to St. Barts in the Caribbean. Later, when we rowed back from *Papingo,* and waved, we realized we would probably never see them again, unless they should decide to sail to the Caribbean (or we to England) someday, which was pretty unlikely.

That night, an unforecast boro boro screamed through. Every boat dragged, and for several hours the cove was filled with maneuvering boats manned by pajama-clad wild men holding flashlights and yelling directions.

Until the west-moving horde comes together at places like Palma, Majorca, or Malaga, Spain, boats go singly between their selected ports, and meet new friends whom, in all probability (if they are LDS sailors heading for an Atlantic passage), they will meet again in Gibraltar. Our own route touched northern Sicily and southern Sardinia.

Like any tourists, we took the trip to the top of Mt. Etna. We drove through Mafia country to the base of the mountain, then took the cable car to the snowline. There, we donned rented army coats (an occasion for hilarious photographing all around) and trudged up through the snow to see the smoke in the crater. Yellow wild flowers grew in the black lava, and the panorama of the Strait of Messina lay below.

Moving on, we stopped at Cefalu, in northern Sicily. It protrudes into the sea, a promontory topped with ancient buildings and a great cathedral. We anchored in behind the headland along with small, brightly colored fishing boats and a few small yachts. At night, we watched the lights of the town as the lighthouse beam washed over us. In the morning, we discovered a French boat lying too close for comfort, and a few cross words were exchanged. Later, we all rowed in together to get cans of water and fuel and to see the beautiful mosaics in the cathedral. They portrayed a simpler, more lifelike Christ than those in the more grand–and more golden–Palermo cathedrals.

Although the guidebook called Palermo the "crossroads of civilization," the seedy waterfront had not been rebuilt since World War Two bombing, the harbor was dirty, and repairmen (at least the refrigeration men) were unreliable. In late August, boats in the harbor included only the hydrofoil *Aliscafi* from Messina, a few steamers, and several yachts, none of which were American. I had visited this harbor by steamer before the war, when it was a credit to the many churches and palaces here. But its storybook backdrop of ragged green peaks, capped by little white villages, remained.

Farther west, Cagliari, on the southern tip of Sardinia, turned out to be a busy and noisy yachtsman's port of call. We docked between a small French boat and a German one whose two elderly occupants played loud church music on their radio all day. During the night a British boat tied to us, and a French boat with a topless girl crew came in. Most boats were being filled with water and fuel and groceries for the journey to the next main stop, in the Balearics. I bought a Timex watch with a silver band with red dots.

After leaving Cagliari, we pulled into a small, wild, but protected Sardinian bay, because of strong, rising north winds. While we were anchored there, we saw the musical German boat enter and then lose her dinghy in the wind. Several of the locals tried to help them retrieve it, but finally they just sailed off and left it, oddly enough.

Odder still, however, was another incident involving the dumping of a large, heavy bag into a secluded arm of the little bay. This was followed by an underwater explosion, much underwater study by a diver, and several husky men on shore, and, much later, by an onshore conference, a last look, and, finally, a retreat from the area by car—a Mercedes. The finale of the kidnappings Sardinians are noted for?

After a two day, two night rolly sea voyage from Sardinia, our first stop in the Balearics was Port Mahon, capital of Minorca, reportedly considered by Lord Nelson the best harbor in the Mediterranean (he also lived here with Lady Hamilton). Two kind people advised us where to dock. They were waiting for the same German boat we had seen in Sardinia. Then, when we wanted to continue on, we encountered Minorca's special brand of weather—strong, northerly mistral winds that meet the warmer Med winds from the south in black thunderstorms that stand solidly between Minorca and Majorca.

Three of us—one bright yellow French IOR (international ocean-racing rule) boat, brilliant against the black thunderclouds, a smaller green boat, and ourselves—spent an entire afternoon going, first, toward Majorca (which we could see), then retreating as the sharp squalls balked us, then advancing again as each passed by.

Finally, it was dusk and each of us independently decided to turn back for the port of Ciudadela at the southwest end of Minorca. The guidebook warned that the narrow entrance was dangerous in the southwest wind that now prevailed, but there was no alternative. Once through the entrance slot that was wild with waves, the narrow, well-lit harbor opened up like a stage set, with restaurants on one side, where the yachts were moored, and fishing boats on the other.

It was here that an American yacht rebuffed us when we asked to tie alongside for the night, there being no berths left. A local fishing boat welcomed us, however, and pointed out the best restaurant. But the fishermen were not eager to start off in the high winds the next day.

"Mañana," they said. "Mañana."

But the winds were our way, and it would be a fast passage to Majorca. Many westing sailboats get to Palma, Majorca, and simply stay because it is so beautiful. We approached, after a long beat up the bay, at dusk. The sun was sinking in a coral sky behind the black mountains above the city. The city lights were twinkling on, and the magnificent cathedral was lit both within and by spotlights surrounding it. The harbor, inside the stone breakwaters, is crescent shaped and has a palm-lined promenade along its full length. It is crowded with yachts as well as commercial ships. The yachts are berthed in real marinas–run by Club Nautico or Club de Mar–rather than receiving the more typical Med treatment as annoying stepchildren to the commercial vessels.

Palma is a cosmopolitan city with modern hotels, stores, and streets, but has, as well, an interesting old quarter, museums, art exhibits, concerts, a glass-roofed, block-square market for anything from fresh fruits to local leather goods, and a summer climate all year long. In the hinterlands are dramatic mountain landscapes, caves, and underground lakes, monasteries and castles, and, of course, the farm where Chopin and George Sand lived during Chopin's illness.

More importantly, perhaps, to sailors, good boat work is available also, and boats from every country fill the marinas. At Club Nautico, we were delighted to see old friends Leo and Gigi from *Morning Haze.* They thought they had a buyer for their boat, and were eagerly looking forward to purchasing a new boat they had picked out in Italy. They said the Haydens were still in Malta, having not left that summer at all.

Next to us was a ketch, *Alma II,* belonging to George and Dolly

Thompson. He had just retired from the diplomatic service (the "chosen people," he assured us, and he was serious), and was embarking now on the voyage of his dreams. Bill asked Dolly how she liked retirement.

"George retired," she said. "I haven't."

George lent me his *East Spain Pilot,* published by Imray, Laurie, Norie, and Wilson in Huntingdon, England, from which I copied important navigational details for every Spanish port, left out in my own *Down the Spanish Coast,* by Bristow. I had trouble, too, getting a chart of Ibiza, walking miles between marinas and finally calling at a dingy old bookstore where two elderly ladies kept a collection of charts. George had an ingenious device for locating his boat at night. Using a radio control similar to that used for flying model planes, he could turn his spreader lights on and off from the dock. They would be staying at Palma for the winter and would explore all it had to offer.

On our other side was a small British boat, with a frail little girl and her parents aboard. They said their daughter had leukemia. The family had sold everything and bought the boat and would keep sailing as long as the child could enjoy it.

We had work done on the boat in Palma, which nearly resulted in our sinking it in the harbor mouth. After waiting our turn at the boatyard (we had negotiated with two mechanics there, one who could speak a little English and the other who could speak a little French), we had the bottom painted and some repairs done to the head in the aft cabin. Because of the tide, we were launched at five in the morning, while it was still dark. As we approached the lights at the narrow harbor entrance, I heard a strange noise in the cabin.

"Well, look in and see if someone was left aboard," Bill said.

I looked in and saw water lapping over the cabin sole and obviously rising. I took the helm and Bill rushed around looking for the leak. The boat became unstable and I pictured her going down right there, in front of a big ship that was approaching from the other direction. The pumps did not appear to be making much of an impression. Then Bill discovered a valve in the aft head that had not been closed tight and was letting in a two-inch stream of water. He quickly closed it and we circled for about an hour until the boat was stable and empty again. We ran all pumps and engines right away, and none seized up from the saltwater immersion.

As boats moved westward along the Spanish Costa del Sol, their crews were concerned about reaching Gibraltar in good time, about planning what provisions and what new equipment would be needed, and when transatlantic crews would arrive by plane. Sightseeing and socializing were at a minimum. Nevertheless, old and new friends, all with similar goals, turned up in the same ports. It was not time for guests, as their welfare was not foremost in one's concentration. Yet we, not realizing the pressure we would be under here, had signed up a constant contingent all the way to Gibraltar.

Although Spain's southeast coast is a wall of tall condominiums—most built by Germans and Swedes—as one rounds the corner at Cape Palos (where Costa Blanca becomes Costa del Sol), and approaches the naval base at Cartagena, Spain shows her true character—dark and mountainous and remote.

The intervening ports, like small Garrucha, are fishing villages not yet attuned to tourism. Only a few yachts stop here—for provisions—and they must tie among fishing boats and local outboards. Spanish officials met us at Garrucha's low quay with a sheaf of papers to fill out. Later, two small boys from a British boat up ahead called on us and told us they were wintering in Palma. At sunset, the Spanish fishing fleet came in. Some two dozen vessels charged in, dropped stern anchors as they rounded the breakwater, and moved in as close to the fish dock as possible. It was the occasion of the day. Cars roared onto the quay, horns on both boats and cars blew, and voices were heard above it all. In the morning, before dawn, the excitement started again. There seemed to be a race to get out. Boats were lit up, engines churned over, and all pulled at their anchors together—some becoming entangled—with more loud cries. At last, they all motored proudly out like eager terriers.

Cartagena itself is a deep indentation in the mountain facade. It is filled with naval vessels, including some former U.S. Navy submarines (and Lt. Dom Isaac Peral's invention, the first electric submarine, now on blocks). At the head of the bay lies the old and eminent city. We motored in, past an anchored U.S. Navy vessel, the *Suribachi,* and tied up at one of the ubiquitous Club Nautico stations (with an easily spotted red-tile roof).

The boat berthed next to us, a small black sloop called *Endeavor,* was American. They were going east, to Palma, but acted as our guides in Cartagena—for the laundry, grocery store, restaurant, liquor store, post office, and beauty parlor. Later, they invited us aboard to meet the commanding officers of the *Suribachi,* who, in their turn, invited us all to tour the ship on the morrow.

The *Suribachi* was a munitions ship. We were shown deck after deck of tightly packed ammunition and missiles – including nuclear ones. On the immense deck were big derricks to load the ammo, and towers bristling with guns.

"How do you feel about being assigned to an ammo ship?" we asked one of the sailors.

"We feel we're on the safest ship in the fleet," he replied. "We know these missiles are packed so that they can survive a direct hit. We packed them ourselves."

We marveled at their confidence (or at the public relations job involved). For lunch, we were served (in the captain's cabin) BLTs, hot dogs, and ice cream – in true American style. Later, the navigator gave us each some old Navy charts of places like Cuba and Puerto Rico.

Next morning, *Endeavor* went east and *Audacious* went west. We wondered how things would go for them. Herb, a Ph.D. in business, and his small son, Jimmy, were traveling along with Marge, a Ph.D. in psychology. Herb's wife was back in Maryland. It seemed to us that each member of the crew was already high-strung and uptight. They had had a very bad storm off Bermuda, on the way over. Sea cocks had opened, and they had to pump night and day for four days, until the storm subsided and they could make repairs. They seemed to be tired still, but were looking forward to Palma.

At Almeria, farther west, we had an encounter with a red sloop from Nantes, which, unfortunately, we were destined to see again and again. Almeria is an uninviting harbor for yachts, first off. The moles are lined up *with* the wind, which allows the swells to roll right in. Boats rock and rub the tall cement quays where they are tied. We were carefully moored with a protective bank of fenders, waiting (and rocking) for a change of guests. Out of the blue, the red yacht drew alongside, and a heavyset, bearded, elderly Frenchman in shorts jumped aboard with lines and proceeded to tie up to us, though there was plenty of room in front of us at the stone quay. Although we pointed this out, in French, he kept right on and called us selfish Americans, and so on. Quietly, Bill untied as he tied, and maneuvered *Audacious* backward, and tied the Frenchman's lines to the quay. Astonished, he glowered at us. He had not wanted to tie next to the concrete, but did not mind if he squashed us against it.

Each time he walked past us, he muttered, "*Sauvages! Sauvages!*"

Next time we saw him, we had both come into the small port of Motril, where one takes the bus to Granada to see the Alhambra. We did not see him on the bus, which carried us over the dark mountains and high agricultural plateau and on to the Alhambra—the walled Moorish city of delicate, lacy stone buildings and lush garden pools (Robert Louis Stevenson's essays best describe the feeling of this mysterious place).

Next morning the Frenchman left before us, screaming orders to his one crew. He said nothing to us, but when we saw him next time, in Gustavia, St. Barts, in the Caribbean, he was a changed man.

There was one more important stop for sailors before Gibraltar—Puerto Jose Banus. This is a modern marina, encircled by smart shops, restaurants, and hotels. Shipwork can be done here; towns and airports are nearby. They boast of having 320 days of sunshine a year, and many boats stay all winter to enjoy them. But many, like us, simply stop for provisions and to await good weather for the last dash to Gibraltar. Actually, it seemed to us rather a tourist facade, for the supermarket was closed for remodeling, no meat or fresh vegetables were available, the Perkins engine man had no oil filters, and there was no weather information at the marina office. (As usual in Spain, the officials sent us to the daily newspaper, where a small weather map—of yesterday's weather—appeared.)

Fortunately for us, and other Gibraltar-bound boats, there was a boat in the marina—a large, American blue ketch called *Tantra*—with a weather facsimile machine aboard. They graciously invited the rest of us to have a look at the maps. We saw a Bermuda hurricane and a series of low-pressure areas moving eastward across the Atlantic from Newfoundland. We were also able to pick up a few snatches of weather broadcast from Gibraltar itself. They were forecasting easterly gales there. It seemed wise to remain for a few more provisioning and boat-repairing days.

At last, we, in the company of three other boats—one French, one British, and one German—started off in the gray swells for Gibraltar. On our last leg, we were in international company, as we had been throughout our westward trek. Undoubtedly, this year and next, the makeup of the flotilla moving westward through the Mediterranean would include all the varieties of LDS boats we encountered on our voyage.

That day, for our final miles, the wind slacked off when the four of us sailed out of Jose Banus, though the sky was still black to the east behind us. Already, we could see the great rock of Gibraltar, and all day we simply sailed toward it. It grew bigger and more defined, and, finally, we could see the white water catchment basins on its eastern slope and the heavy crowning "levanter cloud," caused by the prevailing, water-laden east (levanter) wind.

Faintly, to the south, Mt. Hacko on the African coast came into view. The Pillars of Hercules stood before us.

Tegula

XII

Gibraltar—World-Sailor Crossroads

Throughout classical times, from at least one thousand years before Christ, the gateway to the Atlantic at Gibraltar, comprising the two great rocks—Calpe to the north, Abyla to the south—was known as the "Pillars of Hercules." The rocks were supposedly emplaced by the Greek hero as a memorial to his journey to obtain the oxen of the three-bodied monster, Geryon, on the tenth of his twelve labors done in penance for the murder of his family.

Actually, the Phoenicians, before that, had named the Strait the "Pillars of Milbarth." Milbarth was their god of the sea and the underworld, and the Pillars were the entrance to his Hades, just as twin pillars also defined the entrance to his temple in Tyre. Later, the Greeks identified Milbarth with Hercules.

Beyond the Pillars of Hercules, Euripides said five hundred years later, "lies the end of voyaging, and the Ruler of the Ocean no longer permits mariners to travel on the purple sea." The Phoenicians, who hoped to keep to themselves the Atlantic trade they had begun to develop, continued and, in fact, elaborated on this myth with tales of the "unending stream of Ocean, which poured away over the world's end." For a long time, no one else ventured outside.

Though a skull of a Neanderthal man has been uncovered in

Gibraltar, and it is said that Gibraltar was once connected to Africa, its history really began in 711 A.D., when the Moor Gebel Tarik (from whom Gibraltar gets its name) captured the mountain. There followed sieges by the Spanish and the Moors until the eighth siege when Alonso de Arcos finally captured it, and in 1502 Queen Isabella of Spain placed it under the crown of Spain. More sieges—by the French, the Turks, the Spanish, and finally, the British—ended with the Treaty of Utrecht in 1713, when Spain ceded Gibraltar to Britain.

Although Spain has never given up her claim to the Rock, the Gibraltarians still, in the 1980s, vote regularly, ninety-five percent to five percent, to remain British. In 1969, Spain closed the border to Spain and has yet to permanently open it again. (On Sundays, relatives may call to one another across the intervening gap. We watched this sad spectacle.) For Britain, it has been a strategic harbor in every war, and it was here that Nelson's body was brought, aboard the *Victory,* after Trafalgar.

Under the shoulder of this impressive and historic rock, we rounded the Europa Point lighthouse and sailed the length of the long harbor that had held so many warships over the centuries. We saw only a few gray naval vessels docked inside now. Behind them, the old town crouched at the base of the mountain, houses climbing only as far as the Moorish castle walls.

We passed the old submarine pens, where docking is free but the climb from the boat to the quay precipitous and the surge uncomfortable. Many yachts were there, however—we could see men up masts, laundry hanging in the rigging, dogs and children playing on the dock. But we circled behind the North Mole, beside the busy airport runway, to Shepherd's Marina. It was already crowded with sailboats of all sizes and all countries.

The Cockney dock master, with heavy dark eyebrows and a beautiful handlebar mustache, directed us to a creaking iron barge tied to the end of the dock. We pulled in, stern first, between a big white British yawl called *Oceanaire* and a twenty-eight-foot new sloop from the United States called *Kelly Down.* Next to *Kelly Down* was the *Christmas Rose,* a Camper and Nicholson boat we had once chartered in Ireland.

We thanked the neighboring crews for assisting us into our mooring and found they too were heading across the Atlantic in a few days—as many as it took to complete preparations. Wandering about the marina, we saw every sort of boat, all obviously in the throes of provisioning, repairing, painting, and installing. There was not much socializing here. There was neither time nor interest in that. There was serious work to do, for everyone.

"But they don't all go," the dock master told us. "You'd be surprised how many boats I have here for sale. A lot come here, work awhile, and then a day comes when they decide maybe they don't want to make that long Atlantic trip after all. Then they quietly take me aside and ask me to put their boat up for sale. Why, I have some boats here that have been for sale for years, and I've never heard another word from the owner."

Each morning he would patrol the docks, greeting the captains and reporting the weather.

"Will be strong levanter winds tonight. Pretty heavy seas and possibly fog in the straits. Better not leave yet," he'd say. Or, "There'll be two days of light, warm easterlies. Pretty good for passage out the straits."

It was only a short walk from here to the top of Main Street–the mile-long commercial center of Gibraltar. The faces we met along the street could not have been much different over the ages. There were the pink-cheeked, proper British, dark-eyed Spanish, black-robed Arab and Moroccan women, Maltese, Italian, and Portuguese fishermen, other native Europeans, and Jews. English was spoken, but most store proprietors were Spanish, except the greengrocers, who were from Ceuta or Tangier. Add to that, then, the seafaring transients of all countries, there to purchase vast quantities of provisions. Expensive items like watches and electronics were on display in shops that in former years must have sold a very different kind of merchandise.

There was one other important inhabitant of Gibraltar–the Barbary ape. A community of them lived high on the Rock, and there is a superstition that when the apes are gone, the British will go. To make sure this prediction would not come true, Churchill brought in reinforcements during World War Two.

Although Gibraltar, even more than Marseille or Malta, is truly a crossroads of the world, the flavor is British. There is a weekly ceremony of the Changing of the Guard before the Governor's residence in the "Convent" off Casement Square, and there are the British flags, the Anglican church, the gardens, and the extensive British naval harbor.

It was easy to pick out the harried sailors. They were weathered, even ragged. They stared straight ahead, looking into the journey to be made, a journey like so many already made, where the edge of danger is reached and death is not far away. Like us, they were hunting down particular boat fittings or engine parts and instruments. Many would be found in the section of ancient winding streets near the marina called "Irish Town." We looked, unsuccessfully, for a valve for our Avon rubber boat, and, successfully, for oil filters. And the others, like us, would be trying to get last-minute repairs. I took our faulty marine clock, for instance, to a clockmaker touted as the world's finest.

"Oh yes, I know all about marine clocks. We've been in this business a hundred years," he said. But every time I came back to pick it up, there was still something more to be done. Finally it was ready.

"I couldn't get it to ring just right," he said. He had evidently been trying to get it to ring to twelve, like an ordinary clock, because, back on the boat, it rang thirty-five straight. We disconnected the chime entirely.

For charts, it was necessary to walk several miles down through Gibraltar's residential area, past the railroad, and into the Navy compound along the harbor. Signing in at the gate, we entered the formal British Admiralty Chart Office. Here, I met the owner of *Venture* (the boat captured by the Cubans) and of *Anarch Wey*—whose owner was an attractive, clean-cut Welsh lad who planned to cross single-handed in this small sloop "just to see if I can do it." And if you find you can't, what then, I wondered silently.

Charts must be ordered by number and paid for immediately, so a period of studying the chart guide (with lots of advice from sailors who have already been there) preceded the purchase. The heavy roll of charts had to be carried the several miles back to the boat. It was also necessary to know when the tide would be favorable in the Strait, but the best clue to this was to purchase the *Gibraltar Chronicle* each day. I had written ahead and placed my order and had been assured all charts but LORAN charts (which were U.S. charts) would be available. They weren't.

Most of the boats awaited repairmen—we, as usual, had called the refrigeration men. Parts ordered for the LORAN from the States had arrived, however, but could not be tested because huge transmitters on Gibraltar used the same low frequency—100 kHz—and they completely blocked out the LORAN. Bill, meanwhile, was busy checking all the rigging, tuning up the engine, and changing the oil, tying storm sails on deck, putting on downhauls and the deck lines for the safety harness, gathering together extra fuel and water containers, and tying them on deck and in the boat.

Oceanaire, next door, had men repairing bent stanchions and a man up the mast straightening out a spinnaker halyard problem. Several of the crew were sewing sails, others were stowing the boxes of food and liquor that overflowed on the dock (barge), and they were waiting for a new shaft for their generator motor.

On *Kelly Down*, on the other hand, preparations had suddenly stopped. Kelly, its owner, had been notified, by ham radio, that he was needed on an oil rig off Libya, so he sold us all his fresh foods.

"Actually, I'm retired, though I'm twenty-eight," he told us, "but they have an emergency."

"Would you mind telling me how you can retire at twenty-eight when it took me sixty years to retire?" Bill asked him.

"Yes. I worked on oil rigs in Alaska, worked up to rig boss, earned good money, but had no place to spend it, so I have enough to keep me sailing and to allow me to buy this new boat—just the one I wanted.

"I told them," he went on, "if they really needed me, to call, and I'd work a month, that's all. At this Libyan job—they lost a rigger—I'll earn ten thousand dollars in that time. That'll keep me going at least a year, and I can always get work when I need it."

He had not gone to college, he told us, though he was obviously alert and knowledgeable. No beardo—in fact with a crew cut, he was pleasant and outgoing.

"College was a waste of time. I tried it awhile. Why, right now I earn more than the Ph.D. geologists on the rig who analyze the stuff we pump up."

They put his boat on a mooring, to await his return. Then he would continue on, single-handed, "or maybe with a friend," to the Canaries and the Caribbean.

Christmas Rose would leave next morning. Stores had been stowed, bedding aired, and laundry done. We had compared paperbacks, and traded a few.

"We'll take it easy down to the Canaries," they said. They were a middle-aged British couple who had done only a moderate amount of sailing, and they were concerned about their children back in England. "We'll explore there awhile...Maybe we'll even stay all winter. Who knows? But the *Christmas Rose* is a good boat. She could go anywhere."

Taking her place was a French boat with a large police dog

aboard, who went wild every time anyone passed the boat. Later that night, I happened to observe two deaf and dumb boys who had been hanging around the docks, baiting the dog, getting him all excited. On another night, he got loose and, while we were having a drink aboard *Oceanaire,* he jumped aboard and finished off a chicken we had for supper, spreading grease all over the cabin sole. He would not leave until I carried him off the gangplank to the dock.

There were lots of dogs, most of them huge. One German boat – another single-hander – had two large dogs that would be aboard all the way across the Atlantic. Another dog, chained to the boat, was so high-strung it whimpered constantly. Surely, not a pleasant dog's life.

From *Oceanaire,* we learned a great deal. This was far from her first trip. Her captain, Alan Williams, tall and graying, owned the boat and chartered her (in the Med in the summer, the Caribbean in the winter) to pay for her upkeep. He could not bear to part with her, though his wife was not interested in sailing and his three grown children now lived in Florida. (His daughter did pay him a brief visit here.) *Oceanaire* was seventy-one feet and required a paid crew of five – two girls and three boys. A tall blond boy, obviously experienced, was in charge.

"My captain has been with me a few years," Williams told us, "but the others come and go. They find a bigger yacht or nicer work or whatever and say, 'Sorry, I'm going to work on so-and-so boat now,' and that's it. We lost one girl on the way here, and we're waiting for another to arrive. It's better to have two girls so they have company. But they're an expense," and he laughed.

He took us on a tour of the boat. In the center were the main saloon, the galley, and laundry (washer and drier!), and the storeroom for meats and frozen food. The crew's quarters were forward, the owner's and passengers' (they would have one this trip, a Belgian) aft. Then we settled down for a drink and the trading of "lies" about our terrible passages and good ones.

"By the way," he said, "if you haven't done your provisioning yet, don't go to Lipton's where everyone goes. It's much cheaper at the warehouse [in Pentana], and they'll deliver the boxes right here."

"Without cockroaches?"

"Can't promise that, but on a big order they'll take a personal check and take off about five percent."

We talked about our projected passages across – they would stop at Ceuta for fuel ("but it's hard to dock there and get away in a strong wind")–and go on to the Canaries and Barbados. We would go direct to the Canaries and on to Antigua.

"You'll go down to the corner and then across?"

The "corner" was the place where longitude thirty-five degrees west crossed latitude eighteen degrees north. I had studied the old sailing-vessel routes in the British Admiralty publication *Ocean Passages for the World* and found they had started off from a point west of Gibraltar, gone southwest to this corner, and then turned nearly west to catch the trades to Antigua. So I knew about the corner.

Williams came originally from Glasgow, Scotland, but he saw it seldom now. He hoped to see his children in Florida later on, he said, and perhaps encourage one of his sons to join him in the charter business.

"But he's an engineer and doing well in his own business," he said sadly. "I'm based in St. Lucia in the Caribbean, and we have pretty good clients now. Most have been with us before, so we know what they like. With a booking agent, you aren't apt to get lemons, though we've had a few of those too."

"In the Med, I work from Cyprus. Non-Greek boats can't charter in Greece, you know. Anyhow, I don't go to the Aegean–too windy and too rough."

Oceanaire had further delays–the generator shaft finally arrived, but it was the wrong one, so there was a new wait. They finally left, after a thorough wash-down and shine-up, the same day we did. We watched them turn off toward Ceuta and hoped we would spot them along the long way across, but we never did. Next time we saw *Oceanaire* would be months later, in Antigua, and Williams was not aboard. His captain was, but the rest of the crew, as Williams had predicted, had changed berths to other boats.

One day before we left, we heard someone call "Hello, *Audacious,*" from the dock. At first we did not answer because usually it was some seedy character wondering if we needed a crew or would take passengers, and we had heard enough tales of psychos, hijackers, and plain murderers to shy away from any such discussions. And it could not be our own transatlantic crew, as they were not due until the weekend. When the call came again, we peeked out and saw Leo and Gigi from *Morning Haze.* Another grand reunion.

"Come aboard," we shouted. "Do you have your new boat?"

"No, the same old boat," Leo said. "The deal didn't go through. We'd made a down payment on our new boat and then found the fellow's check for our boat was no good. He didn't have any money at all, and owed people all over the lot. He finally went to jail. So we had to cancel our dream boat."

"It was disappointing," Gigi said, and we knew it was, especially for her.

"So you're going across anyhow?"

"Well, we thought we'd sail up to Belgium, but it's too late in the year for that, so we have a friend coming and he'll help us on the trip. You need at least two men," Leo said. That would mean only one man on a watch. We were lucky to have two.

"We saw *Mimas* farther back, and *Far Horizons.* They'll be going, but only Doc and the two boys will take *Mimas* across. Nancy and the girls have gone to England and will fly to Antigua."

"Any sign of *Shikama*? Has she already gone across?"

"Haven't seen or heard of her. *Phayet* will stay in Crete for the winter, and I guess *Honeybird* is still in Malta. I'd like to know more about her whereabouts."

Leo and Gigi went back to the "pens," where they had docked, to finish the hundred and one preparations for their transatlantic passage. We did not know it, but it was the last we would see of them, after so many chance meetings.

As we watched boats of different flags come and go, and observed their crews on the streets of Gibraltar, we often imagined that this boat was a "drug" boat, that one perhaps hijacked, another one, like the mysterious trawler in Malta with, perhaps, a bunch of terrorists aboard. But in our American innocence of the real political oppression in much of Europe and the Middle East, we did not guess that the real destination for any of the boats was simply freedom and hoped-for asylum in the West. And we did not know, either, how often this escape route had, sadly, been discovered too soon.

Typifying one of the fortunate escapes was the voyage of a thirty-eight-foot schooner from Gibraltar to Elizabeth, New Jersey. The four Polish sailors who made the trip had been sent from the Lublin Yacht Club to retrieve the yacht in Athens and sail it back to Poland. At Gibraltar, they decided to keep going west. Though not close friends, they were all Solidarity members. One of them had friends in Elizabeth. Each one, they said, independently decided not to return to Poland. Being semiprofessional sailors, the trip was not difficult for them. They were given the amnesty they sought, but they did not exactly live happily ever after. They could only find menial work, and they still had to find a way to bring their families here. But they were not afraid of being sought by Polish authorities. As one member of the crew, Jarek Hruzewicz, said to reporters when he arrived, "What are they going to do, send out a cruiser?"

Later, a Czech, Richard Konkolski, with his family aboard, sailed to Newport, Rhode Island, allegedly (like *Phayet* from South Africa) just to sail in a single-handed round-the-world race, but with the added hope for asylum in the United States. He achieved both. It has become a recognized way to travel—modern cruising boats, well-equipped and sailed by intrepid men *can* open the door to freedom. (And even, as in the case of Haitians and Vietnamese, if the boat is leaky, overloaded, and equipped with only torn sails and a tree trunk for a mast.)

Gibraltar is the starting point for many strange voyages. We watched bearded, sad-eyed loners silently push off to try the Atlantic solo, most of them sailing what Bill aptly termed "world boats"—world-weary ancients, patched up and loaded down with gear tied down on deck under tarpaulins. These are sailors caught up in the sailing life, preferring their own company (one boat we noticed was called *My Way*), and now have no other skills but steering a course, trimming and changing sails, subsisting on meager cold rations, and staring ahead to gauge the oncoming seas, the changes in the wind and weather, the time for a landfall. They long ago lost any relationship with the land (except to pick up work here and there). Probably no one would know, or perhaps care, whether they reached their landfall, and perhaps they take some sort of perverted pleasure in this. For them, the term "boat bum" is a way of life, not a stigma. For many, being alone with the mighty seas provides a spiritual ecstasy that draws them ever on.

Quite different—though surely with some sort of similar inner need to search for one's private holy grail, to do what others cannot and would not do—are the single-handers who race across the Atlantic or around the world in their expensive, high-powered, and sponsored, racing machines. Eric Taberly, Phil Weld, Marc Pajot, Phillipe Jeantot, Robin Knox-Johnson, Chay Blyth, Naomi James. These are highly competitive, knowledgeable darlings of the press. Many have designed their own and others' boats. Ham radio operators keep in constant contact (as did some of us in New England with the 1980 OSTAR racers). Transponders installed aboard automatically record each boat position for the race committee, by satellite. And it was possible, when Tony Lush's *Lady Pepperell* began breaking up, after rolling and pitchpoling in the Roaring Forties during the round-the-world race from Newport, for nearby race competitor Francis Stokes to be notified of Lush's plight, and to, in fact, rescue him from certain death in those cold seas.

One wonders how one would "stack up" if faced with the ultimate disaster – a sinking boat, thousands of miles from land. One would hope to react something like Steve Callahan, a thirty-year-old boat designer and builder from Maine whose boat was stove in, possibly by a whale, after leaving Gibraltar. He was adrift seventy-six days in a rubber life raft, and floated with the trades and currents eighteen hundred miles to Guadeloupe. He endured through a combination of determination, intelligence, and luck – determination, in keeping himself supplied with water from the solar still in his raft, in spearing the dorados that surrounded the raft, in existing through fearful storms and seas; intelligence, in planning his day and arranging his raft to keep a life-supporting schedule and defeat his discouragement and fear (he even suffered a rip in the bottom layer of his raft), and luck, in that his boat, though never seen by ships, drifted to inhabited islands before he collapsed. And because of his ordeal, he told reporters, he felt a new appreciation of life. But he said there was no romance about it.

"I was in a constant state of apprehension," he said.

As to our own plans, we finally felt we were ready to leave Gibraltar. Ship's stores were on board, marked with wax pencil, and stowed. The eggs had been vaselined, fuel and water tanks topped, weather checked with the RAF station at the airport, laundry done, showers taken (hair done). Last-minute purchases were made of MacDougall bread flour and steaks that were supposed to be "restaurant" grade (but later had to be thrown overboard they were so tough).

Our transatlantic crew – Bill's good friend Bill Clarke and his son

Copper, and Sandy Dayton, who worked at the Boston Aquarium—arrived bringing our new Genoa and a box of freeze-dried food we had ordered. And most important, plans were complete to resume daily ham radio contact with Joe Lippert on Long Island.

Without further ado, we set sail for the Caribbean.

XIII

Long Distance Sailing Women

"WANTED: Female companion for Mediterranean cruise in 35-foot sloop. Adventurous cook-crew. Send photo. Mermaids need not apply." So reads the sailing magazine advertisement.

And that pretty well sums up the requirements.

Reading between the lines, as it were, you will come to the conclusion that Long Distance Sailing is a man's world. The female is the adjunct, and she must be operational in *all* her requirements, just as all the boat's equipment, motors, and electronics are.

The boat is the man's castle. Not only does it take him loyally to far corners of the earth without complaining, but it is his domain and he is its king. This is neither criticism nor derision. It is simply a fact. It is what living on a boat is all about. Here is where a man can be his own boss, live up to his own standards, whatever they are. He can go wherever he wants, whenever he wants. He can push the boat and his gear to the limits if he wants. He can always look forward to three squares a day, a warm bunk with his books, his blanket, his pipe, and his woman all within easy reach.

Where does the little lady figure?

It is the word "adventure" that catches her first. Far-off places, with her own home along. Moonlit nights. Blue days, with wind in the sails, the slop, slop of the waves. A nut-brown tan. Carefree. She and the man. And the boat.

"If you'd asked me two years ago how I liked this way of life," Dulcie Hunter of *Sululu ya Pili* had said, "I'd have been completely enthusiastic. Completely."

The woman (LDS-f.) enjoys making her small floating nest neat and clean. She likes putting her stores in convenient, recorded cupboards or under the floorboards of the main cabin. Her towels and sheets, their clothes, their heavy-weather gear, all have their places. A small twelve-volt (or bigger) vacuum cleaner keeps her house clean. She can hang her laundry on her own laundry lines on deck, and it will dry in the wind in a few hours. Meals can be probably a little simpler, and the captain may dry the dishes for her. She can do a little mending. Some ladies bring along sewing machines.

Everything is tidy and homelike, until the frequent times when the boat has to be torn apart for repairs of one kind or another, or for sanding and varnishing, when the boat is overladen with a deep frosting of sawdust.

She even gets used to working at a slant. She has learned to brace both herself and her utensils. She takes pride in producing four-course meals, even including bread or cake or pies she has baked, in the height of storms, when the men come in from the cockpit wet and tired from "seeing the face of God out there."

It is not too much trouble, when a certain utensil is required, to take out fourteen utensils in front of it, which tumble about as the boat plunges, and then to return said fourteen—and repeat the process when whatever was needed in the first place is washed and ready to be stowed. She gets used to the coffeepot bouncing off the stove into the freshly baked pie. Even to finding her bunk under the one leak on the boat, and to hearing a crash in the head, only to find all her toilet articles and little bottles of creams and sweet-smelling things she cherishes, all piled in one heap on the wet floor after an encounter with a particularly tough wave.

She may even take quietly and graciously the order to prepare an especially involved dinner after a long day's sail where she, too, has been on deck sailing, and checking the navigation, and trying to get the weather report just at the time of a sail change, and so on.

As Dolly Thompson on *Alma II* had said, "You retired, George. I didn't."

In a deeper vein, a woman is constitutionally not, has never been attuned to wandering forever. Especially if she has children—

although many mothers are bringing their children along and teaching them aboard, for a time. But most women want to be part of something, part of a continuity and a community. She wants to carry some of the responsibility for making the world, the community, a little better, and not just be a disinterested passenger. The jaded observer of the passing scene is not her part to play—usually.

For the most part (even the most dedicated LDS women admit to these reservations), she prefers at least remaining in one place awhile, getting to know other sailors, becoming part of their plans, their histories, their problems and joys. She enjoys keeping in touch.

But then she finds those friends will sail away, and very often are never seen again, and then are no longer friends. They have gone to other harbors now.

"It has been such fun to know you," the Brookes of *Papingo* had told us in Yugoslavia. "Maybe we'll see you again." But we both knew there was no chance of that. Yet, we will no doubt meet other sailors who will have seen them, in this small world.

It comes as a surprise to suddenly realize that this is all there is. Everything one cares about is on the boat, and the boat is far from home.

"I suddenly realized that my house was sold. What had Zane done to me?" Es Mann of *Flapper II* had asked.

The days go on. There are adventures. There are even terrors. Both the man and the woman learn what every ancient sailor has come to know about handling a boat and dealing with the sea and weather. In working together for simple survival, they grow together. They respect and need one another. Things need no longer be said. Like peasants in simpler, harder times, they understand what must be done without speaking.

But, likewise, the constant sharing together, in these close quarters, magnifies annoying habits, personal odors, and expressions, and the value of lost things of a former life. In addition, the woman, as hard as she may fight against it, becomes hardened and weathered. Though she may be more useful as a sailing mate, she has lost the woman's softness and mystery and loses confidence in the company of those with nice clothes and ample bathrooms.

"In the two years we've been on the boat, I've aged twenty years," Marion Anderson on *Maid Marion* said.

In Gibraltar, I observed the sailing women—in practical, weathered jeans and with windblown hair and sunburned faces—gazing longingly at the London fashions displayed in the store windows. They would stand awhile, looking wistfully, oblivious of passersby. Then they would pick up their market baskets and stride on to their next errand.

I look especially at the young girls, lithe and nubile in their bikinis, enjoying their adventurous life in a man's world on a sailing boat. Already, they are becoming not tanned but burned by the sun; they are hardened by the sea and the storms and they are worn out from their tasks in the galley, on deck, and in the bunk. I am not surprised that they often change boats.

"I was asked to do things on board I had not contracted to do before we left," one of the girls told us.

The woman needs to have an important job on the boat, other than managing the galley and cleaning the heads. She should be the official keeper of the log, or do the navigation or be the ham radio operator. Some are particularly good helmsmen, and they should share in the steering. I do not know any that are better mechanics or sail handlers.

But perhaps the apparent frustrations and disappointments in life aboard a sailing vessel are no greater than those "back home." They are merely a more condensed or concentrated version. Yet, on land there is not the fear in the night as the wind begins to howl, of having the anchor drag, nor the dread that the scheduled long passage for the morning will, even so, have to be made.

Sometimes, it may seem that Ruth's conjugal promise, "Whither thou goest, so also will I go," is carried to an extreme in the LDS life. Yet, there it is. It is the woman's choice—keeping in mind that there is always someone who will answer the ad for an "adventurous cook-crew."

But, glory, who would sacrifice to a stranger the hypnotic living at sea—the changing horizons, the intimacy with eternal forces that direct the motions of sun and sea and winds, the fragile and transitory beauties of light and wind and clouds upon the water, the soothing motion and steady companionship of the boat, not to mention the necessary strengthening of teamwork between husband and wife. Most of the inconveniences and fears are, in the end, only like labor pains, soon forgotten appendages to a greater happiness.

And so, the breakfast dishes put away, the LDS-f. handles the helm as her husband winches up the anchor. The sails are loosened, ready to raise. She reads his hand signals, advancing, backing,

XIV

Caribbean Characters

Most Long Distance Sailing skippers will tell you that the Canaries–to–West Indies run is a "downhill sleigh ride." A recent Cruising Club of America newsletter, for instance, told how one crew was able to sand and varnish and play with birds that hitched a ride along the way, while the trades steadily and lightly pushed their winged-out jibs.

Nevertheless, as we found, it is not always that pleasant. We, too, were following the old sailing-ship route—southwesterly to the "corner" (thirty-five degrees west by eighteen degrees north), where one allegedly meets the true easterly trades and west-going ocean currents and can ride them along the eighteenth parallel all the way to Antigua.

The problem is that, at this corner off West Africa are also born weather phenomena called "easterly waves." In the fall, they are the source of the West Indian hurricanes, starting life here as low-pressure areas swirling counterclockwise and filled with squalls and shifting winds—albeit, punctuated with vivid, often double, rainbows. We seemed to be in the grip of such a wave all the way, with big confused seas ("Himalayas," Copper Clarke called them) that were tiringly uncomfortable, and squalls that called for continual sail drill. At one point, Copper, being the lightest of the crew, had to go up the mainmast in these seas to realign a jumped sheave. (His father, Bill, rigged a network of safety lines and downhauls to him, but Copper accomplished the tricky task with cool nonchalance.)

The temperature in the southern Atlantic is hot, and it is humid. We sweated in our bunks at night. And the sea was empty—a watery desert. No birds. No porpoises, nor whales. No ships, even. Sandy Dayton caught just one fish, a dolphin. This was a disappointment, as he had brought along equipment from the Boston Aquarium to do extensive study of tropical marine life, and had rigged a trolling line each day. One day, we did see the tips of two sails and a freighter, but that was all.

At least we were able to get LORAN positions all the way across, although sometimes it took thirty minutes before a reading came through (this would be a sky-wave reading, which is accurate enough in midocean). We shifted from the Mediterranean LORAN chain—7990—to the Norwegian chain—7970, then to the Greenland chain—7930—and, finally, to the fine United States East Coast chain—9930—that we used to have before the present weaker 7980 chain was, unfortunately, substituted for it. We checked the accuracy of the LORAN with sights on the stars and sun and, close to land, with RDF (radio direction finder).

We were able also to keep ham radio contact with New York, except in one area south of the Cape Verde Islands where, Joe Lippert said, our line of contact passed over the Bermuda Triangle! These messages, as on our way across, came in Morse code, across thousands of miles of ocean, amid the difficulties of strong static and rough seas tossing the boat around, but they brought word to the members of the crew from home.

After our twenty-two days out from the Canaries—days of lonely, stormy blue water—Antigua, tall, green, and populated, was indeed a welcome sight. Porpoises at our bow and tropic birds above led us into the sparkling harbor. We followed the directions in Don Street's *Guide to the Lesser Antilles* to get into English Harbour (though not his detailed description of how to sail a square-rigger in), and dropped anchor among boats of all nations. We, like other newly arrived transatlantic boats, wore a crust of long "midatlantic goose barnacles" across our stern. In fact, it was easy to tell the travel-worn transatlantic boats from the shiny new boats recently down from the States. But I, at least, drank in the smell and sight of flowers, reveled in the flat platform under us at last, and, in the evenings, enjoyed the sharp soprano chorus of the ubiquitous tree toads.

Pourtales Abalone

In Antigua and the other Caribbean islands, we were to add a new cast of characters to our roundup of LDS sailors. And, as usual, there were old friends from Europe and the Mediterranean: *Mimas, Marie Pierre, Far Horizons, Cuilaun of Kinsale, Oceanaire, Janie,* to mention a few.

Antigua's English Harbour is geographically and by reputation the center of yachting in the Caribbean. You can find an example of most – but not all – Caribbean sailing types here. It lies more or less equidistant between Puerto Rico and Trinidad. It is the most protected harbor in the Antilles and, perhaps starting with the aura of Admiral Nelson, it has kept an elitist atmosphere. Thanks to the Nicholson family (originally from England), the dockyards and outbuildings have been restored and now there is also a Nelson Museum, a true English inn (with steel-band music in the evening), and a sail loft. But it is the company of boats there that sets it apart: from Bermuda Race winners to single-handed circumnavigators to chartered square-riggers to SORC (Southern Ocean Racing Conference) boats to the *America* to LDS boats from ports around the world.

We backed into the quay between an English boat called *Sea Boot* (her captain was formerly with the RAF) that we had last seen in Cagliari, Sardinia, and *Spirit of Delft,* a sleek blue Dutch charter boat (registered in Spain). A few boats away was the old campaigner *Ticonderoga,* now taking charters but kept as beautifully as ever by her charter crew. A little farther along was our old friend *Mimas* (they were still threatening to sell her).

Beyond *Mimas* was an eighty-five-foot powerboat that was later impounded for weeks because one crew member was found with marijuana cigarettes. Just in time for Christmas, the fifty-five-foot, bright-hulled *Cuilaun of Kinsale*, owned by Ian O'Flaherty, came in from the Atlantic.

Christmas in Antigua! It meant not only an unnatural Christmas in the tropics, but Christmas among strangers—except for our new family of LDS sailors.

It was a jolly holiday for the LDS group, however. Parties were organized so that each crew had its own responsibility. One boat supplied Christmas cocktails (ours—we had twenty-five aboard). Another (a Canadian trimaran called *Conalee*) served a main course to which all invited contributed a dish. Another had dessert and coffee (*Mimas*), and so on. The parties overlapped all around the harbor until late at night, when high-spirited dinghy loads searched the harbor for their own boats in the darkness.

Also, at Christmastime each year, the Nicholson family serves champagne on the dockyard grounds to all crews in the harbor. It is a dress-up affair (some come in costume) and boats are in the "dressed-ship" mode as well as having Christmas lights and trees. Our daughter, Peggy, and I roamed the prickly hillsides for plant material for a tropical Christmas wreath, which we hung on the mizzen boom. The native children came round each evening singing Christmas carols (and looking for a few coins of appreciation). Next day (Boxing Day), there is a sailing race outside the harbor.

Of course among the young and well-paid charter crews, partying was not confined to Christmas. In fact, that was why, a few days after the holidays, the Gillies took *Mimas* and their five children out of the harbor at dawn one morning.

"We have to get the children away from this hedonistic influence," Nancy said. "Everything is just too available, and they're influenced by this attitude of simply enjoying yourself."

"They feel put upon if I ask them to do a little work," Doc said. "They act stoned all day."

The owners and captains were having trouble, too. The crew on *Ticonderoga* was down to captain and one hand. *Oceanaire* was the same.

"Antigua is the place where crews look around and decide some other boat will be easier or more prestigious to work on," *Oceanaire's* captain told us. "Of course, there's no denying that charter crews work hard, but, on the other hand, they knew when they signed on that certain things had to be done when chartering—cleaning, cooking, planning, repairing, varnishing, painting—as well as sailing the boat in every kind of weather."

Then the delivery crews steal away some of them, too – especially the girls. For delivering high-class yachts – usually brand new ones – means simply sailing them from here to there and living the life of Riley (in Tortola, we saw one crew of six having a fine, formal, candlelit dinner in the cockpit of a forty-eight-foot Swan they were delivering), while collecting a substantial fee for doing the very things the crew would most like to be doing. ("I'd rather be sailing," the bumper sticker says.) Their only problem is a deadline to meet.

Both charterers and delivery crews, however, as well as LDS owners who are short-handed, must be as alert here as in the Mediterranean for would-be pirates who might ask to be taken on. There is not as much danger of piracy "on the high seas" now as there is in taking aboard the obsequious lad (or lass) who asks just to be taken to, say, St. Thomas. Anything can happen, so credentials should be carefully checked. (We did pick up one pirate, inadvertently, in Antigua – a small, ineradicable brown flour bug.)

At least boat repairs are no problem in Antigua. Besides a good shipyard, the islanders are eager to work. And there are no union hours. One charter boat, *Ocean Mistral*, was due in St. Martin, but ran into trouble – several troubles – the day she was supposed to leave. A pump in the head leaked, flooding the starter so that the engine could not be started. The leak was repaired, and "Cap," Antigua's electronics expert, worked until two in the morning, until he got the starter operating for them. They then started right off for St. Martin – even at that hour. (The other trouble involved one of the crew. When the men had the floorboards up, while repairing the leak, she was loading on boxes of provisions and did not notice the open floor. She fell through and broke her ankle. She decided to go along, cast and all.)

For other errands – filling propane gas bottles, getting traveler's checks, and so on – it is possible to go to the town of St. John by bus. This is usually a battered VW van, with seats. It stops wherever someone is waiting for it. I once got on when it was already crushingly filled with blacks and was told succinctly by the driver, "Get to the back of the bus!"

As we sailed among the tall, solitary, lush islands of the Caribbean Antilles chain, we met quite a number of what seemed to be a typical Caribbean type of LDS sailor – ones who, for the moment, were shorebound. Although these sailors still lived aboard their

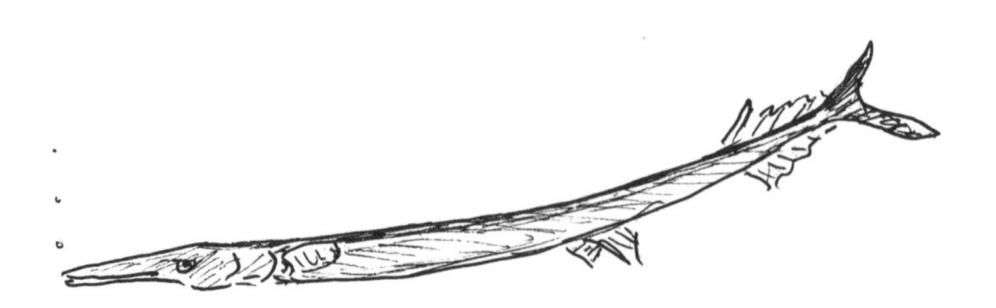

boats, they (like the Petersons aboard *China Clipper* back on the French Riviera) now worked ashore. An Englishman who worked as an electrician in the Antigua shipyard, for instance, had brought his wife and small daughter and cat across the Atlantic in a twenty-four-foot sloop, going by way of Dakar, Senegal, and Natal, Brazil, where it was only eighteen hundred miles across instead of thirty-six hundred. Bill asked him how he liked Senegal.

"Well," he said, "you don't have to enjoy it for it to be an experience." He might stay at his job in Antigua now for several years, before moving on again.

We found the greatest number of "grounded" LDS sailors in the Virgin Islands. There was the lady in the American Express office who still lived aboard but had been working in Charlotte Amalie for six years. They still cruised around a little, she said. Then, the people who ran the Anchor Marine store there (where we could buy *any* chart) were originally from North Carolina. They had been sailing around the Caribbean for four years when they decided to open the store in St. Thomas. They still lived aboard, too.

Another type was Jorgenson, the "Wizard." He lived aboard a Controversy sloop called *Warlock*, moored in Soper's Hole in Tortola. His wizardry was in alternators and generators. He had learned about them by taking apart his own faulty alternator repeatedly and rebuilding it. Gradually, he found himself doing the same for others and decided to go into the business. Now he is sought after. He came aboard our boat in old blue jeans, a wool cap, and a full blond beard. His language was punctuated with strong four-letter words.

"Shit," he said, after looking over our ailing electrical system. "You'll *never* be satisfied with that electrical refrigeration in the tropics with this setup."

"We have the windmill to keep the batteries up," we pointed out.

"You need an alternator the size of a friggin' truck Delco, then.

But that won't fit in here without putting in bigger plates and I don't do that. I do have the Delco Eighty-eight. I had it for a drug-running boat that was impounded last week." He put in the biggest alternator he could and did some rewiring. It has been working fine ever since.

"I'm what you could call a fugitive from the executive world. I left all that and came down here. Now, I work only the winter six months," he said. "Then, I sail for six months. Why, in our present lifestyle, me and my woman, we can get along on six thousand dollars a year. Shit, what more could you want!"

Now contrast the Wizard with another Caribbean type—the jet-set, nattily dressed sailor who cruises the Caribbean from Trinidad to the Virgins in very large yachts. They have other boats at home—home being Texas, Chicago, New York, Europe—as well as twin-engine planes with which to shuttle between the two. The Internal Revenue Service seems to think all yachtsmen fit into this category, but actually it is a small segment (though it is being swelled by the huge, fast boats bought with drug money).

Rather typical was a Swan-48 berthed next to us in St. Thomas, owned by an Englishman who did not really care for sailing. He had a paid crew of four who moved the boat around to convenient places for him. Next stop was to be Cannes, in time for the film festival—only the crew was still waiting for a check to pay the marina bill.

We concluded that the sailors here did not worry much about marriage. A typical case was a forty-foot yawl. Two couples were sailing her back to the Chesapeake for a friend. Neither was married. Bill happened to ask one of the girls, who was British, if her husband was also from England.

"Oh, he's not my husband," she said. "He's my mentor." Although she had a college education, she was supporting herself by sanding, varnishing, and delivering boats. Her real concerns were for the environment.

Nor does anyone worry about nudity, particularly in Martinique and St. Barts (St. Barthelemy), which is fast becoming a center for the young and for racing. Its only restrictions on nudity are limited to bicycling. A black Mystic-30 anchored near us one day in Martinique, while Bill was varnishing. Although the skipper wore shorts, shoes, and even a hat, his lady came up on deck and washed her hair without a stitch on.

"It ruined my varnishing for the day," Bill said.

We met quite a few, like the professor aboard the *Aurora Borealis* and the Psychology of Communications teacher aboard the trimaran *Sannu*, with his wife and small children, who were taking a year off from teaching duties "to reconsider life." They were able, somehow, to make the necessary financial arrangements to do this. With similar outlook, were three fellows aboard a trimaran who helped us tie to the quay in Samana, Dominican Republic. We asked them aboard for a drink later, and they brought with them enough chicken and rice for supper for all of us. They told us they had met by chance and decided to join forces and sail around for a year or so. They would stop and take charters and go diving, and stay long enough to get to know the people, they said.

"One of us is a poet, another is an artist, and the third is from Wales," they explained.

We met Bill County here, also. He was a trim young man on a small motor sailer named *Tara*. He was in Samana by himself because his crew had decided to leave without warning. He had an interesting story to tell. He had sailed in different parts of the world, racing, and happened to be traveling as a tourist in Greece when he read that one of the Greek ship barons was looking for a crew for his racing sailboat. He had applied for the job, and gotten it.

"I was lucky," he said, "as I only had thirty dollars left at the time. The boat was to represent Greece in some races in the Med and to stir up interest in sailing in that country. So I was fed and housed all summer while we raced. We made a good showing, came in third, and got medals from the government. The man was so grateful he gave me passage back to New York on one of his freighters. I landed there with just ten dollars."

When you see a square-rigger in the Caribbean island ports, it is not always merely a tourist charter boat. Often, boats like *Apple-*

dore, close to us at anchor in Ponce, Puerto Rico, can be oceanographic vessels with students living aboard. *Appledore*, named for one of the Isles of Shoals off Portsmouth, New Hampshire, where she was built, carried twenty students and three in crew in her sixty-foot length. One girl (wife of the first mate) did all the cooking. She started at four in the morning, getting the stove hot and baking bread. When we spoke to them, she had about had it, after a full year, and was planning to take a vacation.

As we sailed up from Martinique, through the velvet, green, mountainous islands of the Windward-Leeward chain, and through the Virgins and past Puerto Rico and the Dominican Republic, we inevitably saw old friends.

In Gustavia harbor, St. Barts, we were surprised to see the Frenchman from Nantes, who had called us *"sauvages"* back in Almeria, Spain. There, in the crowded Gustavia Post Office, we practically rubbed stomachs trying to pass one another. There was a brief smile, and, later, as we dinghied by, a small wave. Perhaps having his wife aboard this time made the difference. We saw the two of them often walking along the shore, examining the flora and fauna. And they, like us, seemed concerned about a beautiful white bull tied ominously to a post beside the abattoir at harborside.

At St. Martin (or Maarten) we came across *Tantra*, whose weather-facsimile machine we had been able to view in Puerto Jose Banus in Spain. In the Virgins, we found the Irish *Cuilaun of Kinsale* in one of the Peter Island anchorages. (There are no lonely anchorages left in the Virgins, thanks to the millions of charter boats.) At Nevis, we had a chat in the dark with Phil Weld, whose *Rogue Wave* was anchored nearby. She had recently raced from France to Martinique. And we got word from a former crew of *Oceanaire* that the Welsh lad who had started across the Atlantic in *Anarch Wey* had decided to turn back in the Canaries, and had returned safely to Gibraltar.

In Charlotte Amalie harbor in St. Thomas, which was crowded with sailboats and five big cruise ships, we saw the MacGregors and *Far Horizons*. They arrived alongside by dinghy and we talked a long time. After Jim and Bill compared notes on the best way to bleed air from their diesel engines, Jim told us that they were rather undecided about their future plans. First, he did not know whether to simply sail to Florida and start anew there, or to continue the long sail to the Panama Canal and up the coast of Mexico and California to his waiting real estate business. Elsie, on the other hand, just wanted to get the children back to the United States and in school.

"We're kind of tired of cruising, I think," Jim said, "of pushing on from port to port, country to country. It's the long ocean passages that tire you, although we've set up a pretty good schedule. The small boy takes the helm for one and a half hours at dawn and dusk and once during the day. The little girl sails a few hours during the day. Elsie sails seven hours and I take it for ten—except in bad weather when I'll do most of it. We don't change sails unless it's absolutely necessary. And then, we've been living on tuna fish pretty steadily now..."

We talked about harbors in Puerto Rico (which has become a mecca of sailing, particularly the East Coast) and in the Dominican Republic, and then Jim and Bill got on the subject of insurance.

"I don't believe in insurance," Jim said. "It's just a form of gambling. I figure it's not worth insuring for the little losses—sails, a bump here and there, thefts. It would only be worthwhile to insure the whole boat. But I look at it this way. The whole family is aboard. Everything valuable is aboard. If the boat goes, we all go together."

As it turned out, Jim was to regret that decision.

Our path led north. We would leave the fabled Caribbean beaches under their leaning coconut palms, the cloud-shrouded rocky peaks, and the boisterous trade winds—and with them our last contacts with foreign cultures—French in Martinique, Guadeloupe, St. Barts, St. Martin, and Haiti, and Spanish in the Dominican Republic and Puerto Rico. We would now sail for the long string of low islands and cays that stretch seven hundred miles northwestward to the Florida straits and the Gulf Stream. The Bahamas. The *Bajamars*, Ponce de Leon named them in 1513, meaning *shallow waters*, for, except for the most far-out islands, they sit upon an ocean bank only barely awash with the most diamond-clear, hypnotic waters in the world.

Cry for the Bahamas

The wind in the casuarinas
  whispers, moans
  for the ghosts of the Bahamas,
the dry mangrove scratches along the white beach,
  sighs
  for the ghosts of the Bahamas.

Reaching barely higher than the sea surface,
  with soil too thin
  and luck much less
  such struggle here
  such sadness
  such striving
  in these small islands in a chain
  built by tiny animals
  on mountaintips
  in the shallow seas, the *Bajamars.*

Only the simple life has ever worked here,
  the Lucayans came first
  and Arawaks,
  warmed, fed, content
  with fish, sun, sea, and fruit
  and with their native Gods,
  they set the pace, the only one that works.
Works, yes, but this was not to last
  (what does, that's simple, good?).

From across the seas came Spaniards in sailing ships,
  other Gods, they innocently thought,
  and welcomed them,
  bowed down, in fact, surrendered all
  and for this they were, in time, exterminated.

No more did Lucayan or Arawak
  enjoy this land.
Of them the casuarinas whisper now
  the mangroves sigh along the white broad beach.

It was only gold the Spaniards sought
  not fish, nor sun, nor fruit
  nor warmth
  nor native Gods.
And so, for a time,
  in the contest
  between all the fighting navies
  the land was blood-stained
  the reefs strewn with foundered ships.
Then, once again,
  the islands stood alone and silent
  only the ghosts
  and the casuarinas whispering
  and the silent beaches waiting,
  with one, here and there,
  a few of the simple folk
  who could persevere and survive.

Yet, in these lonely, narrow islands
  stretching a thousand miles southeast
  lying there in the sun
  and sparkling water
  abounding in the basic needs of life,
  surely an oasis could be found
  (or so many thought).
So, while some came searching a sanctuary
  others came for more illegal practices.

And a pattern evolved
  that has not changed
  it is the curse of the Bahamas.
Time and time again, it repeats:
  it is the struggle between
  colonizers, planters and builders
  and law breakers, smugglers, and killers.

For the lonely cays
  the shallow sounds and quiet beaches
  the crystal waters and the warm sun
  all favor both pursuits
and both pursuits bring wealth
  but wealth of a different kind
  than the simple content
  of Lucayan and Arawak.

Here is a primeval good and evil struggle
   played out in
   an Eden land in the azure sea.
The casuarinas know, whispering there
   and the wide white beach
   staring back at the silent bright sky
   and the ghosts multiply
   of hopes lost, of starts thwarted.

Look only at the history
Let history speak for itself:

First, colonists landed, to make a new start
in a bright new land,
but the ground was hard
the water scarce
and only the hardy remained.
Then Spaniards leveled the capital in Nassau.
Later, pirates did the same,
but pirates, scavengers of wrecks and privateers
brought in wealth
and Nassau rose again, but tainted now.

The colonists planted cotton
then sisal
then sugarcane
then pineapples, potatoes, and citrus.
They built plantations throughout the islands
but brought in slaves
   (there were no more Lucayans here to work
   they had been killed off long before).
But they brought little wealth
for everywhere, it seemed, had better markets
than the Bahamas.

Then the slaves were freed
and England ruled the archipelago.
Wars were fought
blockades were run
and wealth came in again
and the simple contentment
the simple secret of the Bahamas
the sun, the fish, the fruit
the stories and the songs
were not enough.
The native Gods were silent
though still the casuarinas whispered in the wind
along the stark white beach beyond the mangrove.

Another try, and still another, followed,
amd many colonists left for good
leaving the slaves
now masters here.

And the time came
to look again at the living things
in the shallow seas
that were there still
had always been
since Lucayan times
and long before.

So Bahamians now
(it was now a nation)
made boats
and went upon the seas
for fish, for crawfish, for turtles
and, especially, for sponges
and for many years
they prospered
from the produce living there.
But once again
it was not to be
for sponges began to die
beset by a fatal scourge
and with them
died an industry
and men again went hungry.

Then again rose the pirates
the ship wreckers
the rum runners and smugglers
hiding in the coves till night
then streaking out
with contraband
collecting enormous sums
(though quite a few got killed).

* * *

Now look again.
How has it changed in the present day
  it has not changed at all
  nor ever will
  forever will be the ghosts
  forever the Bahama curse
That is what the casuarinas say
that is why the mangrove's sighing...

XV

Bahamas Easy Life

Although the trades weaken in the Bahamas, the dangerous northers are stronger and more frequent than farther south. Sometimes, the wind goes from a lazy ten knots up to seventy knots in the minutes it takes for the black roll clouds of the front to slide, unhampered, across the open banks and low islands. Tides ebb with great strength from the banks, and the unpredictable currents that move among the outer islands are little understood.

Of the seven hundred islands and two thousand cays spread over the banks, only a small percentage are inhabited, and even along the inhabited ones are unseen, unused pockets and coves still frequented by smugglers and renegades.

Yet, these flat slivers of prickly scrub, with their white sand beaches, cast a languorous spell. The beaches are often bordered by low palms and soft, whispering casuarinas that nearly hide settlements of small, pastel-colored houses where the most friendly of island people live. Once encountered, the Bahama islands will draw the casual cruising sailor back again and again. Even so, only the more experienced test themselves against the wilder, outermost cays with their strange currents and poorly charted coral reefs.

Most LDS sailors first approach the Bahamas from the Caribbean, as we did, from the south, taking the long, often stormy and rough passage from the Dominican Republic. (It was here that we battled an unforecast wind of sixty knots for this 190-mile stretch, with a dead engine.)

In contrast to the tall, rocky Antilles, easily perceived from miles away, the low Bahamas first appear as a smudge on the horizon, then a series of smudges, and finally as a solid line of land. Sometimes, a single tower or casuarina tree, taller than the land, is the first thing seen. Then, as the island materializes, it seems to recede, until, finally, when only a mile or two away, it is truly there.

Great Inagua, the most southerly Bahama island, does not cater to tourists nor to yachtsmen, except as a port of entry. It is in the business of producing salt for the Morton Salt Company. The company has extensive salt pans and loading docks that are noticeable by day because of a brilliant white mountain of salt and by night because of the bright lights on the docks. On this island, also, is the Bahamas' only flamingo preserve. And although the neat, tidy village appears fairly primitive, good facilities, repairs, and necessities are available. The only boat protection at Matthew Town, however, is a two-hundred by two-hundred-foot man-made basin, which must be evacuated whenever the weekly mailboat arrives. (Inagua does have an excellent radio beacon on 376 kHz with call letters ZIN that reaches out 120 miles, and the 7980 LORAN chain begins to be completely accurate here.)

It was here, in the Inagua basin, that we encountered a new kind of traveler on the sea – the Haitian "liberty boat." Along with a few yachts, three heading north, two going south, this old vessel, which had seen better days – many of them – was moored in the corner of the basin. It was piled high with pieces of discarded metal. Sheets of metal and old rusted engines, boxes, tools, you name it, were tied precariously anywhere there was space. There were several families living aboard. They cooked their food over an open fire in a container on deck. It was reported that they were waiting for parts for their engine transmission. But every evening, when the local Bahamians were off work at the Morton Salt Company, they brought food and drink down to the Haitian boat, and the smoke from the fire and the celebration spread over the small basin. We did not discover where they planned to sell the metal, but it was easy to see that they were happy to be in Inagua.

Later on, off Hatchet Bay in Eleuthera, we met another Haitian boat. It was heeled over, sailing hard on a twenty-knot breeze, traveling toward us at about seven knots. As we passed, we saw that it was manned by half a dozen Haitians in short pants and with bright cloths around their heads. Jet-black arms shot up and wide smiles showed white teeth.

"Liberté! Liberté!" they called out, and sailed on.

The other boats in the Inagua basin were waiting for the wind to ease off and finishing errands and repairs. Two–one American, from the New Jersey town where I used to live, and the other from Toronto, where our daughter lives (the small-world syndrome again)–were owned by retired couples, like ourselves. And we were to find that this was the predominant group that sailed the Bahamas these days. This was where they ended up, and where they sailed until they could no longer get around on deck. Many of them were in their seventies and eighties and still were doing the thousand-mile grind down the Intercoastal Waterway fall and spring, and weathering northers and tricky reefs of the Bahamas all winter. Most had sailed all their lives, but some were neophytes.

Marion and Gordon Anderson on *Maid Marion* originally came from Scotland, but settled in Toronto in 1952 where Gordon became president of a large machine-tool company and commodore of the local yacht club. His son now ran the company, but both he and his wife still received salaries. Their boat was an Irwin-43 and Gordon was a very able captain. They had been traveling with *Widgeon,* the New Jersey boat, since the Virgin Islands, Gordon acting as a sort of protector to *Widgeon,* a forty-two-foot Gulfstar, whose crew was less experienced.

Burton and Dude Barnard of *Widgeon* were childhood sweethearts who had married other people who later died. They had then married, and purchased the boat to start a new lifestyle. *Widgeon* was bigger than anything Dude had sailed before. He kept having trouble with an overheating engine and a loose jib. Then, coming from Haiti to Inagua, he had somehow got into Cuban waters, where he was set on the right course by a Cuban Coast Guard boat. Then he lost his anchor off Matthew Town in Inagua. So it went.

The three of us started off together one evening for Acklins Island. We had been warned that a strong northwest wind could sweep into the Inagua boat basin right over the breakwater, and that "no rope you have on board could hold your boat." Since a northwest wind was forecast, we had to leave. We tacked all night. Sometimes I talked to passing freighters to alert them as to our presence (most were Cuba-bound). By daylight, we could see Castle Island lighthouse and the lay of the islands off the tip of Acklins. (This lighthouse, like many in the Dominican Republic, is often not lit, making it important to plan your arrival there after dawn, as the channel between it and Mira por Vos shoal is too narrow to depend upon the LORAN alone.)

After a radio consultation, we decided to head for Acklins' Jamaica Bay anchorage for protection from what was now a strong northeast wind. (Being retired, and LDS sailors with our homes afloat, we could afford to wait here awhile.) We anchored in the turquoise water of the bay, the water so clear it appeared to be only a few feet deep, and saw no house, no person, not even another boat. The island was merely a strip of soft green scrub, and the boats appeared to be floating in air above the water. Gordon helped Dude with his jib, which had ripped on the way and was dragging in the water, finally putting on one of his own.

For another week, we traveled together, which is a common practice in the Bahamas (is, in fact, advised, in the light of alleged hijackings and murders—but more of this later). This means each move is preceded by a consultation and is governed by the speed of the slowest boat.

At Clarencetown, on the eastward, or windward, side of Long Island, we spent four days waiting for some letup in the wind. Enjoying the company of other boats, we spent the time (besides the ubiquitous errands and repairs and searches for engine parts) playing cards in a local bistro, and talking about the sailing life. Although a few other boats were in the harbor, two of them singlehanders going south, it was a temporary stop for most on their way north or south. The friendly villagers, ranging from jet black, through the browns to white, were delighted when weather kept the sailing visitors harborbound. There is a road the length of Long Island which runs through small settlements and also modern marinas, like Stella Maris. Clarencetown is noted for its two twin-spired churches (they can be seen from far offshore) designed and built by Father Jerome, a converted Catholic priest who built other Bahamian landmarks.

One day, at the end of a rousing game of "Stop the Bus," Burton Barnard announced, "When we finally get to our home on Harbour Island [Eleuthera], it is going to be the last time I step aboard a sailing boat, any sailboat. This boat is for sale."

"Well," said Marion Anderson, "while I've been aboard *Maid*

Marion—that's two years now—I can tell you I have aged. It's really a man's paradise, this boating life, not a woman's."

Yet two years later, we were to see the Andersons again in Nassau, still aboard *Maid Marion* and in good spirits. The Barnards were in their house on Harbour Island, with *Widgeon* lying at anchor in the harbor.

"She's really for sale now," Burton told us then, again.

As we worked up into the colorful Exuma Cays chain, to lonely Cat Island, the long and fertile Eleuthera (the first island to be colonized, in 1649), and on to Nassau, we began to meet the horde of charter boats. But among them were Long Distance Sailing people of several types.

First, the retirees. They tended to cluster around either Georgetown, Great Exuma, or Marsh Harbour and Man-O'-War Cay in the Abacos. The Exuma LDS sailors enjoyed diving, snorkeling, fishing, and the true, relaxed Bahamian life (the men were usually bearded). The Abaco denizens seemed to be yacht club émigrés who had been serious ocean sailors elsewhere in former days.

Then, in contrast to them, were the young couples—some with young children, some with tiny, old boats, others with new, expensive ones. (One of those with a small boat they were "restoring" turned out to be Gordon Anderson's son and his wife.) None of the young couples seemed to be making life easy for themselves, yet they were completely enthusiastic about the sailing life, for the moment at least.

We met a couple aboard a lapstrake sloop called *Friede,* for instance, who had sailed from Portland, Oregon, and *sailed* through the Panama Canal. Having no engine, they propelled themselves in tight corners when there was no wind, with a long sweep oar at the stern. *Eastward,* on the other hand, came from Halifax, Nova Scotia. She was twenty-four feet overall, with large canvas bags of equipment lashed on her decks, and the pleasant young couple aboard her had been sailing for two years. The girl had a sewing machine on board and did sail repairs to keep them going. We were anchored together in Marsh Harbour, and when we asked them aboard, they could not come as they were busy "jarring" their fresh food in order to keep it without refrigeration. Earlier in the day, we had watched frantic rowing back and forth from boat to town dock. It was a matter of lost glasses, presumably left ashore and later found on board, but there seemed to be no recriminations at all.

"We think we need a bigger boat, after two years," they told us, "and we're on our way to Florida now to start building it. We've already laid out plans."

We met another couple, while awaiting a wind change, in Royal Harbour, Eleuthera, who were sailing a small, black boat called *Freddie.* They were from Mattapoisett, Massachusetts, and he was a nuclear engineer who specialized in "start-ups." He worked only long enough to finance his sailing. Bob had met Susan in Spanish Wells, and they had joined forces. *Freddie* was named after Bob's father, who had advised him not to put off taking a sailing trip until he was old. His father had done that and missed out because of cancer.

The Sifton family, from Canada, with small daughter Kimberly, lived aboard a new Westsail called *Kahlib.* James had been an executive in an advertising firm and had become disenchanted with the "establishment" life. His trip was to be a year or more, until he decided what to do with his life. Kimberly, he and his wife, Suzanne, said, had been very shy when they left but now was perfectly at home with the strange children she met from other boats. (Recently, we heard James sold the boat and is working in Canada in environmental work.)

Another family from Canada were sailing a fiberglass sloop named *Alegria*. We were anchored beside them in Little Harbour, Abaco, where we both had come to see sculptor Randolph Johnston and his studio. They had built their boat–it had taken them eleven years–from prize-winning plans from a magazine, they said. They had also totally rebuilt a Mercedes engine for it.

"When you have no money, you have to do it the hard way."

They had three children aboard, all of whom were completely at home on the boat. One, in fact, had climbed up the mast while we were talking.

Many young men come to the islands, bum around awhile, get a little work in boatyards and, finally, buy an old boat which they plan to fix up and sail, possibly, around the world. Matthew Janes came to Man-O'-War Cay and worked at Albury's shipyard, side by side with the Haitians. He arrived aboard an elderly sloop called *Amantha*, belonging to a young girl and her two children. He had signed on to help her sail the boat to the Abacos, and had had a rough, stormy trip of it.

"I learned to respect the sea on that trip," he said. "I honestly thought we would never make it. The boat was leaking, we ripped a sail, the engine wasn't working right, and I wasn't sure where we were. Then suddenly the storm quit, and we found our way here. Someone on Man-O'-War took a fancy to the girl, though. She's gone now. I don't know where."

So he picked up work in the shipyard (his specialty was fancy lettering for the transom) and learned marine carpentry skills from the Alburys. The Albury family, along with the Sands, Weatherfords, and others, are descendants of Royalists who fled the Carolinas after the Revolution and settled in the Abacos. Their boat building is famous throughout the islands. Matthew bought one of the Man-O'-War Family Island racing sloops, *Rough Waters*, and, in his spare time, built a cabin on her, cut down her racing mast, and worked at converting her to an ocean cruising boat. Then the law was passed barring non-Bahamians from work (or, rather, the law began to be enforced).

"I'll go back to the sea now," Matthew told us. "I've served in the Navy (in fact, he had known our friend Peter Zendt in Newport then), and my father is a tanker captain. I'll work for a year aboard a tanker and get money to buy the engine and pay up on what I owe. I'll sail across to Belgium then, I think. There's a girl there I want to marry." He showed us a picture of a smiling brunette. He had picked up the Bahamian patois in his speech, and, as he talked, his past experiences became ever more impressive. Now, his boat lies at anchor at Man-O'-War, aired and watched over by his friends, and awaiting his return from the sea.

Other young men have been caught up in the lure of the easy money in the drug trade. For a while, they prosper spectacularly—boats, planes, gold jewelry, girls. Then one day, when they become disenchanted, they find out that, once in, the only way out is by death or prison.

Pirates and smuggling have always been endemic to the Bahamas, of course. Actually, drug trafficking is a disease that has spread to the entire East Coast now, thanks to the increased activity of the U.S. Coast Guard in Florida. We were checked and photographed as we entered Bahamian waters at Inagua by a big red helicopter from the U.S. Coast Guard cutter *Dallas*, for example, and drug busts are daily Florida events now, with the help of highly technical U.S. Navy radar planes and balloons. But drug dealers present little danger for the ordinary sailor these days, as it has become big business—big airplanes, big powerboats, big guns. Except for chance encroachments on their operations, the only killings are among themselves (and good riddance).

The most highly publicized murder of innocent sailors was just such a case—where the sailors surprised the traffickers in action and then spread the word by VHF radio. It was not a wise move, yet it is certainly understandable that one's first reaction be to "report on" traders in the stuff of future ruined lives for their own criminal self-enrichment. Obviously, the traffickers do not consider themselves in this light. Rather, a typical case is a young customs official in Marsh Harbour. He had acquired for himself a new house, large car, boat and airplane, and a gold pin (allegedly worth twenty thousand dollars) which spelled out "Try God." But one day, he confidently called Florida on his VHF aircraft radio to say he was coming in with a "load." This time, his call was intercepted by the U.S. Coast Guard, by whom he was met instead of by his accomplice.

There is some harassment and thievery by the natives, as there is anywhere in the States. The Siftons in *Kahlib* were chased one night by a high-speed boat that shone a searchlight on them. As they got no answer to a query on emergency VHF channel 16, they realized this was not the Coast Guard and that some kind of action was necessary. Any course change was followed immediately by the searchlight as the boat grew nearer. When it was within range, therefore, James took out his shotgun and shot out the searchlight. The boat turned and disappeared.

Once, we anchored in remote Current Island anchorage—no house, no person, no boat in sight, only the wind across the low island and the swift current boiling past the hull. Then, an old fishing boat with three islanders aboard anchored only yards away, watching us with binoculars. Bill and my cousin Anthony Wharton brought the shotgun on deck, just to be seen. We kept watch all

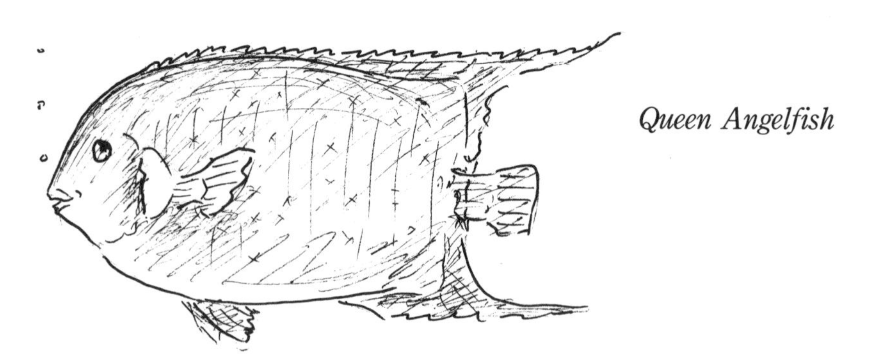

Queen Angelfish

night, with lights on, picturing some nasty happening if the fishermen should have a few drinks. But the boat was gone before first light. They had probably been keeping watch on *us* all night! You can overreact, but it does no harm to have a weapon on board, just in case.

Probably the biggest sailing event in the Bahamas is the Family Islands Regatta at Georgetown, Great Exuma, in April. It began as a contest between working sloops from each island. Nowadays, the sloops are honed down and raced seriously. Like Chesapeake Bay log canoes, they carry tremendous sails and large crews who scramble out on hiking boards to keep the boat on even keel. The island crews wear bright shirts lettered in the boat's name and wool caps. The boats are at anchor, sails furled, on the starting line. At the gun, they must pull up the anchor and the sails to start. The competition is keen and vociferous. The streets of Georgetown, for the occasion, are lined with hastily built stalls for selling shirts, fruit, beer, and programs, and there is music and dancing in the streets.

The spectator fleet–boats congregate from all over the Bahamas–is over one hundred strong. They have cookouts and partying ashore, and stay for a week or more.

Most of them dillydally among the Exuma Cays on their way home, braving the turbulent passages from Exuma Sound between them to reach the silent, haunting, shallow bank beyond. It stretches in shades of brilliant green and turquoise to the horizon and provides a protected way northward along the ninety miles of cays.

Many of them keep in touch, daily, by ham radio on what is known as the "waterway net"–on 7268 kHz at 0745 to 0845, plus a listening watch throughout the day. Run by some dedicated ham operators in Florida, it gives weather forecasts, checks on overdue boats, takes "float plans," and provides a chance to simply chat with other cruising sailors.

There is another important group of native watermen plying the Bahamian waters. They are the interisland mailboat captains.

Captain Theopholis Stewart is owner and captain of *Bahamas Daybreak*. He carries mail (not all interisland boats are awarded a mail-carrier license) and supplies from Nassau to Spanish Wells and, through the "Devil's backbone" passage across the northern Eleuthera reefs, to Harbour Island. He allowed us to ride with him, in his wheelhouse, free of charge, over to Harbour Island, where we planned to visit the Barnards from *Widgeon*. Although Harry Kline's excellent *Yachtsman's Guide to the Bahamas* gives a detailed picture—full of x's for rocks, and dots for extensive reefs—of the tricky Backbone passage, we felt that with strong north winds and only a sailing yacht's auxiliary engine, it was more prudent to go by mailboat.

The *M. V. Bahamas Daybreak* is eighty-five feet long, but she was not always. Captain Stewart, a very dignified black gentleman, said he bought her up on Lake Erie after World War Two, and had her lengthened—a section put in the center—to the proper size for the interisland job he had planned for her. (He was an islander, from Bluffs on Eleuthera.)

"She's steel, and I could see she was a true vessel, but not quite big enough. So I bought her and had her renovated. It took over a year and then I brought her down myself, through the Erie Canal, the Hudson River, and all down the coast. It was a hard trip, but I had no money left to pay someone to do it.

"She's beginning to pay her way now. The main thing is to keep her in good shape. A boat that is always breaking down is no use to you."

He pointed out the secrets of the Devil's Backbone—where you came in very close to shore, how you kept clear of underwater reefs and fast currents there, and pushed over sand bores off the Harbour Island pier.

"I anchored some red buoys along here to help the sailors, but the greedy Spanish Wells guides [they charge forty dollars] removed them all."

We returned with him later in the day—after he and his two man crew had off-loaded cartons of food and soft drink, household equipment and appliances, plants and paints, and even a tractor which had to be run down an improvised gangplank, while the vil-

Limpet

lagers stood around watching and giving advice.

"I'm a religious man," he told us, "and I often pass the time here in the wheelhouse singing my favorite hymns." For the rest of the return trip, he first hummed, then sang in a full and accurate baritone his favorite Baptist hymns. It was a moving accompaniment to the strong seas breaking against the vessel as we pushed into the hot afternoon sun.

Around this time, the first of May, an exodus of visiting sailors begins, leaving the islands to the natives (and Floridians). Up at Man-O'-War cay in the Abacos, the indigenous colony of retired LDS owners was looking northward.

During the fall and winter, they had been living the Bahamas easy life. Aboard their cruising boats, they kept busy doing odd jobs of repair and refurbishing, their wives housekeeping their small, compact worlds. Former racing sailors, most of them, they did not merely stay at the dock or at anchor but scheduled small trips to fairly close by islands to explore and swim and enjoy. To keep from feeling, perhaps, guilty at taking it so easy, they usually planned at least one longer trip to the southern islands—often to the Family Islands Regatta. It was wise to plan conservatively, though. There was always the danger, as they got older, of accidents. For example, Arthur Rowe had lost his wife overboard at night in the Atlantic from their fifty-five-foot schooner, *Morning Star*, and Captain Sparks had succumbed to an arm mangled while anchoring during a storm off Great Guana Cay in the Abacos.

All the life events touched this little community—sickness, marriages, births (we knew of the arrival of our daughter's baby through ham radio), deaths. For indeed it was a community—a community of friends with similar backgrounds, and now similar outlooks. And these ties seemed to have become stronger than those to friends known longer but who were still tied to land interests that had now become obsolete for the retired LDS community.

Here, for example, are some typical members of a community of retiree Long Distance Sailing people.

Dale and Charlie Conlon had been living aboard *Limmershim*, a big ferro-cement ketch of their own design, for eighteen years.

"It's our only home," Charlie said, "and we've sailed to some thirty countries and islands, here and in Europe and South America."

Sam and Anne Bell had been cruising aboard forty-four-foot, Tripp-designed *Blue Angel* for ten years, but were, at last, planning for a house in Maryland.

Sally and Bob Baylis from Connecticut, on *Fantasy,* another Tripp design of forty-two feet, were formerly in the tobacco business. Lifetime sailors, they regularly sailed south in winter and north to Maine in the summer.

John and Tommie Boden on *True Hope* (they had just given up their motor sailer for a trawler) had had a Connecticut machine shop that produced special stampings for the electrical business. Now, they enjoyed exploring quiet, remote cays and doing serious shelling.

George and Dorothy Atterbury from Pennsylvania on motor sailer *Whimsie,* Nancy and Bronson Farnam from Connecticut on *Sans Terre,* and Flossie and Sunny Gibbons-Neff from the Chesapeake's Eastern Shore with racing yacht *Prim* and trawler *Blue Star,* were all retired farmers who had always been active in yachting circles. The whole Neff family, in fact, were ocean-racing sailors–Bermuda, transatlantic, and even America's Cup racing.

Virginia and Dixon Downey traveled on the European canals in their converted barge, *Mon Reve,* in summer, and from their Bahamian island, Cornish Cay, in the Abacos, on *Peppercorn,* in winter.

Jean and Bill Schroeder built their steel ketch *Topaz* for their retirement (he was an engineer, she a teacher) commuting from their Michigan home to Canada. It took them seven years.

The Howes from Cape Cod had their forty-foot Bahamian ketch *Frigate Bird* built in Man-O'-War by "Uncle" Bill Albury back in the early sixties. It was built of heavy madeira wood and ballasted with stones, and had very shallow draft, just right for extensive Bahamian sailing.

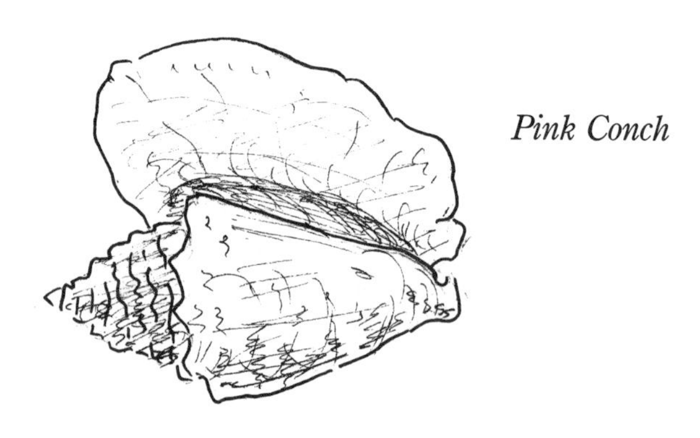

Pink Conch

Betty Hetzel, from Connecticut, a widow in her seventies, still sailed her Pearson-35, with friends for crew, all the way to a Bahamas winter each year.

An aimless life? Perhaps, but there was always the next port to reach, and the important rigging to do. There were the other "expatriots" with whom to share an evening's cool drink in the cockpit at sunset, and to trade outrageous lies about past exploits. There were the pleasant friends in the Abaco settlements who kindly came to consider the sailors as friends. And there was the dark tropical sky full of stars at night, and the waters so clear and shining they could not be believed in the daytime. And the boat, ready to go anywhere she was asked to go.

XVI

Denouement

For the moment, our encounters with the Long Distance Sailing people will end here. But in every sea, there are, even now, new sailors hoisting sail and letting go of the land in heavily laden craft that will take them on, perhaps, an endless voyage into this new way of life of the long-distance sailor. Many are even set to explore more remote and forbidding waters of the planet–in Antarctica, Greenland, Siberia.

We have met, along our journey, sailors as different as any of the persons met in the course of a lifetime. We have sailed along with Corinthian ocean-racing sailors of every country, with their top-notch, completely equipped yachts. We have anchored among the home-built boats, with jerry-built equipment and gray-beard owners who have learned everything the hard way, and are not loath to tell all who will listen how it should be done. There have been boat builders and doctors, engineers and poets, farmers and stockbrokers, retirees and young families. And along with all of these who have turned to sailing and living aboard a boat as a way of life, as an end in itself, were others who earned their livelihoods in long-distance, longtime sailing–the young, ambitious charterers and boat-delivery crews, the bargemen, the fishermen, the interisland boatmen, as well as the ubiquitous smuggler and hijacker.

Living in the small worlds of our own boats, we have made friends whom we shall not forget and whom we shall also expect to meet again, unexpectedly, in other harbors. We have known them, shared their problems and joys, and will keep track through the grapevine that can shrink the LDS world very small.

For example, the MacGregors. Finally, a long, sad letter reached us that described their trip back to California. Elsie wrote: "We lost our yacht *Far Horizons* when we hit a reef at 11:15 at night six miles off the San Blas Islands of Panama.... She pounded all night.... Every twenty seconds we were picked up by waves and slammed down on the reef.... Water was coming into the main cabin and she began to break up.... We took to the life raft and drifted (we had lost the oarlocks and the motor would not work) toward an island, until a Kuna Indian approached in a large dugout canoe with a motor. We lived for five days with these primitive Indians, before reaching Panama by motor island schooner. We lost everything with the boat, but, thank the Lord, not our lives." They are now in California, where Jim has a boat and is planning a long single-hander. Elsie is simply happy to have the children back in school.

News reached us that Al and Lou Hayden sailed their *Honeybird* to Israel, where Al became involved again in his old career. He was designing airport complexes for the Israeli Air Force.

The Cloughleys, from the Northwest Territories, have completed their circumnavigation in *Nanook*, and written a book about it.

We heard no more from the Vanderbents on *Shikama*, but did send a message with an Australian sailing to Fremantle. We never saw *Morning Haze* and the Colfs couple, but learned, through the Gillies of *Mimas*, that they made it across the Atlantic and had arrived in the Caribbean. We have had no word on *Phayet* from South Africa. Nor have we seen the Hunters on *Sululu ya Pili*, though they had recently been seen in the Caribbean, too.

The Gillies sold *Mimas* in Florida, on their return, but Doc often turns up on some new Canadian sailboat on his way to Florida. The older boys kept their interest in sailing and have been doing yacht delivery. Nancy, however, is adamant.

"People who quit the world to sail forever on a sailboat are merely cop-outs, failures at everything else. Who cares," she says to Doc, "whether you've been transatlantic? Big deal. Only some other crazy sailor."

Hum Barton of *Rose Rambler*, dean of British cruising sailors and founder of the Ocean Cruising Club of Britain, died in his eighties shortly after winning the Blue Water Medal for his exploits.

We keep seeing *Cuilaun of Kinsale, Tantra, Marie Pierre*, and the Caribbean LDS fraternity. We even saw, recently, in St. Thomas, a light green Nicholson ketch we last saw in Rhodes, Greece. Then, her engineer owner kept her spic and span, but she had come upon bad times, evidently. Now, she had green grass growing on her bottom, ends of sail blowing in the wind, and no one on board.

When dangers like strandings on reefs, fatal hull and rigging failures in storms, run-downs by ships at night, fires, man overboard, critical illness far at sea, await them, what reason do the Long Distance Sailing people give for choosing their lifestyle?

Along our journey, we asked that question, and our answers were varied.

You remember that many sailors told us, particularly the young or semiyoung with small children, that they had left their homes and jobs and gone to (returned to) sea to "reconsider my life." Some had never sailed more than a small boat before. What they wanted to leave behind was frustration, meaningless detail, no freedom. Some were disgusted with the present goals of government. Many of the young spoke of a lack of future with nuclear holocaust hanging over us all, and they wanted to see the world before it was too late. They thought seeing it from a "home afloat" would be economical as well as satisfying the current "back to nature" urge. Some even wanted to join the terrorist organizations. Some just thought it would be fun, before settling down.

Walt Whitman, in his "Song of the Rolling Earth," exhorts the young to "walk out with me toward the unknown region, where neither ground is for the feet nor any path to follow." And Buckminster Fuller, the nation's late guru, theorized that people make the greatest discoveries when they "venture into outlaw areas, where survival is dependent on ingenuity and efficiency."

These are the drums the young are marching to.

With single-handers and those young at work in chartering or boat delivery, perhaps the reasons are simpler. In the boat businesses there are adventure, challenge, new faces, and good remuneration. The single-handers, on the other hand, subscribe somewhat to Mallory's reason for climbing Everest—"because it is there." But, also, there is the desire to "do it my way."

"Solo sailing," Tony Lush told a newspaper reporter before he left on the 1983 round-the-world single-handed race, "has the advantage of always having good company and reliable crew aboard. There's good, dependable navigation, the cooking is excellent, and I find the crew always gets along well with the skipper."

For every sailor, there is a certain hypnotism in the steady passage of the sailing boat through the sea – propelled only by the tall sails filled with earth's wind. The rhythm of its meeting the waves and the sound of the water broken by the bow falling back along the hull is a music that will forever lure the sailor to the sea. As the sailor guides the boat, it comes alive. It calls for adjustments and sensitive hands. It answers with renewed speed and zest, or, if the seas and winds are angry, with strengthened determination and gallantry.

Homer describes Odysseus' ship in her rush for Ithaca and home:

> "How a four horse team
> whipped into a run on a straightaway
> consumes the road, surging and surging over it!
> So ran that craft and showed her heels to the swell,
> her bow wave riding after, and her wake
> on the purple night sea foaming.
> Hour by hour
> she held her pace; not even a falcon wheeling
> downwind, swiftest bird, could stay abreast of her
> on that most arrowy flight through open water..."

With this common feeling for the sea and the craft comes a fraternity among sailors. If, out across the empty reaches of the ocean, a call for help is heard by another sailor in his small, frail boat, it is not unusual for that sailor to turn his bow in the direction of the call, and, somehow, miraculously sometimes, find the boat in trouble.

Back in that round-the-world race, when Tony Lush pitchpoled in the Roaring Forties, he had slim hope of being found, let along rescued. Yet, a ham radio operator in Australia heard his Mayday (from "m'aider") and relayed the message to a Newport, Rhode Island, ham, who notified the Race Committee. The committee knew that the nearest boat to Lush was Francis Stokes's *Moonshine*. Relayed back, the message reached Stokes, despite static and weak signals. He immediately turned back toward Lush's last known position. Somehow, among mountainous, rolling graybeards and in the piercing winds and cold, he found Lush's foundering boat and was able to pick him from the sea and get him aboard his own boat.

Sailing in foreign waters, American sailors cannot call the Coast Guard, and there is always the fear that a boat answering a call may be a "pirate." Fortunately, this is not usually the case, though it is prudent to make sure. Rather, it is more apt to be another example of sailors helping one another—just as they do in harbors, when there is trouble with engines, pumps, rigging, or whatever.

Although the sea is held to be utterly indifferent to the mortals that venture out upon it, often a mysterious source of help, unexpectedly and silently, helps sailors in desperate situations—a kind of guardian angel that takes pity.

For example, sometimes, when you are approaching a new harbor in some foreign land, late in the day, with the wind dying, or, perhaps, increasing to a gale, the smallest shaft of sunlight may pick out of the haze, only momentarily, the light at the entrance. Some think dolphins have appeared to show a ship the way to land (there is one story of a sailor drifting in a life raft being pushed to shore by dolphins). Or, as it happened when we searched for Mizen Head on our foggy landfall in Ireland, a fragment of cloud broke away just long enough, but no more, to give us a glimpse of the headland that was there. I have had the same experience flying, when searching for the airport in the clouds below.

More recently, strong following winds and currents brought us close to Castle Island in the Bahamas while it was still dark. The lighthouse was not lit, there was no moon, and the passage between the island and the Mira por Vos shoal was narrow. Then, a light appeared astern. It was a ship going faster than we were, but on a lower course. I called him on the radio, to check our position. Right away, he answered, in broken English, giving me his position, and said, politely, "The light is not lit, but you have passed it. Keep on your course, you will safely pass the shoal."

He proceeded on into the night and disappeared. Why had he arrived at just that frightening moment?

You have observed, along with us, the growing number of retirees living aboard sailboats and moving about the Caribbean and the Mediterranean—and even among the south sea islands. For many, this is the dream toward which they strove throughout their working lives. For others, the availability of comfortable, safe, and well-equipped cruising boats and the promise of adventure and a certain amount of challenge, have answered their need for a new direction. Still others, looking for less challenge, turn to live-aboard sailing for economic reasons.

In these pages we have noticed the new friendships that form among the retirees who have left behind or outgrown the active roles of their middle years. And we have seen, as well, that as their sailing forays become less ambitious as time goes by, they can, in this way of life, slow down with dignity. They are still captains of their ships, still keep them shipshape, still go out upon the sea with skill and knowledge and pride.

Is it so strange that we are drawn again to the primordial seas of our origin? That we have a deep desire to shake off the noisy and frustrating impedimenta of modern life, and long to return to the elemental sea and the sky, the call of the seabirds, the timeless passage of the constellations along the ecliptic?

"Come with me," Archibald MacLeish said, in his poem "1933,"

> You have only to cross this place
> And launch ship and get way on her
>
> Working her out with the oars to the
> Full wind and go forward and
>
> Bring yourselves to a home:
> To a new land: to an ocean
>
> Never sailed. Not to Ithaca,
> Not to your beds—but the withering
>
> Seaweed under the thorn and the
> Gulls and another morning...